GOVERNMENT PROCEDURES AND OPERATIONS



# POTENTIAL EQUITY IMPACTS OF ROAD PRICING

## GUIDANCE FOR STATE, REGIONAL, AND LOCAL GOVERNMENTS

# GOVERNMENT PROCEDURES AND OPERATIONS

Additional books in this series can be found on Nova's website under the Series tab.

Additional E-books in this series can be found on Nova's website under the E-book tab.

GOVERNMENT PROCEDURES AND OPERATIONS

# POTENTIAL EQUITY IMPACTS OF ROAD PRICING

## GUIDANCE FOR STATE, REGIONAL, AND LOCAL GOVERNMENTS

RAQUEL BOLES
EDITOR

NOVINKA

*New York*

For permission to use material from this book please contact us:
Telephone 631-231-7269; Fax 631-231-8175
Web Site: http://www.novapublishers.com



**LIBRARY OF CONGRESS CATALOGING-IN-PUBLICATION DATA**

ISBN: 978-1-63117-111-6

*Published by Nova Science Publishers, Inc. † New York*

# CONTENTS

# PREFACE

Addressing potential equity issues is often vital to obtaining the support needed to implement road pricing projects. In order for road pricing projects to succeed, the implementing State, regional, and local agencies must understand equity issues, develop mitigating measures, and articulate the issues and mitigation strategy to both decisionmakers and the public. This book provides a guidebook for state, regional, and local governments on addressing potential equity impacts of road pricing; and discusses income-based equity impacts of congestion pricing.

Chapter 1 – This guidebook is designed to assist transportation agencies to better assess and mitigate perceived and potential equity impacts of road pricing projects on local communities, commuters, and system users. Addressing potential equity issues is often vital to obtaining support needed to implement road pricing projects. In order for road pricing projects to succeed, the implementing state, regional, and local agencies must understand equity issues, develop mitigating measures, and articulate the issues and mitigation strategies to both the decision makers and the public. This guidebook will help agencies understand and communicate both the horizontal and vertical equities of their road pricing policies and projects.

Chapter 2 – This equity primer was produced to examine the impacts of congestion pricing on low-income groups, public opinion as expressed by various income groups, and ways to mitigate the equity impacts of congestion pricing

In: Potential Equity Impacts of Road Pricing ISBN: 978-1-63117-111-6
Editor: Raquel Boles 

*Chapter 1*

# GUIDEBOOK FOR STATE, REGIONAL, AND LOCAL GOVERNMENTS ON ADDRESSING POTENTIAL EQUITY IMPACTS OF ROAD PRICING*

*Marwan Madi, John Wiegmann, Emily Parkany, Myron Swisher and Jennifer Symoun*

## ABSTRACT

This guidebook is designed to assist transportation agencies to better assess and mitigate perceived and potential equity impacts of road pricing projects on local communities, commuters, and system users. Addressing potential equity issues is often vital to obtaining support needed to implement road pricing projects. In order for road pricing projects to succeed, the implementing state, regional, and local agencies must understand equity issues, develop mitigating measures, and articulate the issues and mitigation strategies to both the decision makers and the public. This guidebook will help agencies understand and communicate both the horizontal and vertical equities of their road pricing policies and projects.

* This is an edited, reformatted and augmented version of the United States Department of Transportation, Federal Highway Administration publication, FHWA-HOP-13-033, dated April 2013.

# 1.0. Purpose and Introduction

## 1.1. Introduction

Addressing potential equity issues is often vital to obtaining the support needed to implement road pricing projects. In order for road pricing projects to succeed, the implementing State, regional, and local agencies must understand equity issues, develop mitigating measures, and articulate the issues and mitigation strategy to both decisionmakers and the public. These steps are necessary because equity is a paradox: what may appear equitable in one dimension can be construed as inequitable in another.

Much has been learned over the past two decades both from successful projects and those that have not reached implementation but from which best practices can be derived. As a result, an equity guidebook is needed to provide agencies interested in implementing road pricing strategies with tools and methodology to properly address equity issues.

***Early Consideration of Equity Issues Is Critical to the Success of Road Pricing Projects***

Equity concerns have been raised in the development stages of most proposed road pricing projects in the United States and abroad. Experience from projects that have reached implementation has shown that with proper consideration of equity and associated mitigation measures, road pricing projects can be successful. Most projects currently in operation have found pricing scheme acceptance levels to be similar in low-, mid-, and high-income groups.

Recent projects have illustrated the importance of appropriate and timely consideration of equity in the ultimate success of major pricing projects and programs. As part of Washington State DOT's (WSDOT) Urban Partnership Agreement, the agency proposed to impose variable electronic tolls on all lanes of an existing non-tolled floating bridge on SR-520. The existing bridge was in need of replacement and there was not adequate funding available for the project. Such a strategy – tolling of existing non-tolled infrastructure to raise revenue for its replacement – has been considered for many projects nationwide, as our transportation infrastructure ages. However, no other agencies have succeeded in making the case to the public and decisionmakers to take this controversial step.

The WSDOT designed a strong public process to help build support for roadway pricing. A tolling implementation committee was established in 2010 to gauge and build public support and to provide guidance to the legislature. The committee succeeded in demonstrating the need for replacing the deteriorating existing bridge and the resulting mobility benefits of doing so to all users of all income levels. The WSDOT worked with the regional transit agency to initiate a substantial increase in express bus service within the SR 520 corridor for several months leading up to the start of bridge tolling. This created an expanded transit market and helped to reduce traffic diversion effects. In addition, WSDOT provided traffic mitigation funds to local agencies to assist in dealing with the expected traffic diversion. Toll collection began in December 2011 and has been received favorably by the public.

A key lesson learned from these congestion pricing projects is that equity issues should be addressed at the earliest practical phase in project development because those who perceive inequity are likely to object to the project's implementation.

Road pricing projects of all kinds (tolling, HOT lanes, congestion pricing, parking, and vehicle-miles traveled (VMT) fees) are expected to become more important in the United States over the next decade. The U.S. Federal gas tax and many State gas taxes are not tracked to inflation. As an increasing percentage of the vehicle fleet switches to higher efficiency hybrid, plug-in hybrid, and non-gasoline modes such as electric, the gas tax revenues will continue to decline and will be insufficient to cover operations and maintenance costs. In this financial environment, funding for new infrastructure, needed to keep pace with expansion of vehicle miles traveled in congested cities, is even more scarce. To deal with this lack of funds, States may begin financing transportation projects more heavily from the sales tax, but this is highly regressive by any vertical equity measure. Schweitzer and Taylor stated, "Using sales taxes to fund roadways creates substantial savings to drivers by shifting some of the costs of driving from drivers to consumers at large, and in the process disproportionally favors the more affluent at the expense of the impoverished."[1] Alternatively, State and local agencies may employ road pricing more extensively, such as current legislative changes being promoted in Oregon, and will thus need to quickly address vertical equity issues.

***The Need for a Road Pricing Equity Guidebook for State and Local Agencies***

In today's challenging financial and political environment, State and local transportation agencies need a common reference both to understand and to explain potential road pricing equity issues in common terms and using a consistent set of measurements. This guidebook will greatly help them understand and communicate both the horizontal and vertical equities of their plans or policies to reach a common understanding among key decisionmakers and stakeholders. This is especially true today as policy initiatives for sustainability, the environment, efficiency of provided services and congestion or demand management are key objectives for many transportation organizations. In the wake of the recent economic downturn, the funding and maintenance of our infrastructure will continue to dominate our debate for years in the future. These funding debates could raise further equity concerns.

## 1.2. Purpose of Study

Many road pricing projects and systems have been successfully implemented, despite experiencing setbacks in the concept development and planning stages with respect to equity concerns and other issues. Often, the perception of equity imbalances has been a significant issue introduced in the environmental review process, however it has been successfully mitigated through careful and thoughtful programs.

In order to assist transportation agencies to better assess and mitigate perceived and potential equity impacts of road pricing projects on local communities, commuters, and system users, the Federal Highway Administration (FHWA) developed a *"Guidebook for State, Regional, and Local Governments on Addressing Potential Equity Impacts of Road Pricing."* The guidebook:

- Provides comprehensive procedures and guidance to State, regional, and local agencies as well as decisionmakers and concerned citizens to follow when considering road pricing projects to ensure that equity is appropriately and adequately addressed;
- Focuses primarily on time-of-day variable pricing as it may be applied to cordon and area-wide pricing, facility pricing (including high occupancy toll (HOT) lanes, express toll lanes, and traditional toll roads), and parking pricing.

- Is built upon:
  - A comprehensive literature review of existing road/congestion pricing equity research and applications;[2]
  - A series of interviews with government staff, academics, private sector representatives, and other subject matter experts knowledgeable about road pricing equity; and
  - A workshop held in Washington, D.C. in October 2011 to review and finalize the guidebook. The workshop was attended by road/congestion pricing and equity experts including government officials, researchers and academics, as well as private sector representatives.[3]
- Includes two road pricing scenarios/case studies identified by FHWA. These include:
  - Scenario 1: Agencies considering implementing roadway congestion pricing strategies for the first time.
  - Scenario 2: Agencies considering road pricing expansion along their network.

The remainder of the guidebook includes the following:

**Section 2.0: Congestion and Road Pricing Strategies – Illustrative Scenarios** describes two examples of relevant road pricing strategies that will be used throughout the guidebook for illustration purposes.

**Section 3.0: Congestion and Road Pricing Equity – Definition and Factors** provides a comprehensive review of equity concepts that should be considered during congestion pricing discussions.

**Section 4.0: Incorporating Equity in the Transportation Planning Process** describes how agencies should integrate equity indicators in transportation and project planning processes; and how to measure congestion pricing equity impacts both qualitatively and quantitatively.

**Section 5.0: Evaluating Equity at the Project Level** presents a methodology that can be used to measure congestion pricing equity impacts both qualitatively and quantitatively.

**Section 6.0: Strategies to Address and Mitigate the Impacts of Congestion Pricing** provides a comprehensive approach for minimizing the impacts of tolling and parking pricing initiatives on local communities and system users.

**Section 7.0: The Role of Communications in Congestion Pricing Initiatives** presents a summary on communications methods and strategies to address equity when seeking to successfully implement pricing projects.

**Section 8.0: Recommendations and Next Steps**

**Appendix A: Glossary provides a detailed definition of key equity terms, types of equity, mitigation terms, key policy definitions, and other useful terms.**

**Appendix B: Detailed Review of Potential Remediation Strategies for Congestion Pricing Equity Impacts**

**Appendix C: Bibliography**

## 2.0. Congestion Pricing Strategies – Illustrative Scenarios

As discussed in Section 1.0, two illustrative scenarios were identified during discussions with FHWA staff and discussions with subject matter experts, academics, practitioners, and State and local agencies. These examples were deemed relevant for the purpose of this guidebook and include the following case studies:

- Scenario 1: Agencies considering implementing roadway congestion pricing strategies for the first time.
- Scenario 2: Agencies considering road pricing expansion along their network.

### Scenario 1: Agencies Considering Implementing Roadway Congestion Pricing Strategies for the First Time

In this scenario, it is very important to consider equity at all stages of the project to ensure a successful implementation and lay the groundwork for future road pricing projects in the region. In a region where travelers are unfamiliar with road pricing, communications of the project objectives, needs, and use of the funding are paramount. Equity issues should be analyzed and presented proactively and as early as practical. It can be difficult to gain public support, especially if there are perceived equity issues that are not being adequately considered.

Incorporating equity considerations into the earliest stages of the planning process is critical in that equity issues that arise for the first time during later phases tend to delay or block project implementation.

## Agency and Region New to Pricing

For the purposes of this guidebook, we will think in terms of an agency and a region new to pricing as follows: county X has two urban areas separated by a 12 mile long, eight-lane freeway. Ten years ago, the county widened the roadway from three lanes to four lanes (each direction) by adding a High Occupancy Vehicle (HOV) lane alongside the three general purpose lanes. However, the HOV lane has been consistently underutilized, leaving the highly congested general purpose lanes adjacent to the low volume HOV lane. The agency is considering an HOV to HOT conversion, which will allow carpools (HOVs) and buses to continue to use the HOT lane for free but charge a fee to ineligible vehicles to use the lane.

# Scenario 2: Agencies Considering Road Pricing Expansion along Their Network

In this scenario, the original facility should be well established and evaluated, and there should be an awareness of the current road pricing conditions in terms of effectiveness, acceptance, and an awareness of pricing. Few equity-related problems are being caused by or perceived within the current HOT lane system. For this scenario, expansion can be considered either by extending the length of the facility, expanding the capacity of the existing facility, expanding into a network of priced roadways, or implementing a cordon pricing scheme.

Expansion can be highly rewarding and very effective in dealing with the growing challenges of congestion and a limited ability to expand freeway capacity due to construction costs, right-of-way constraints, and environmental and societal impacts. This scenario is very much related to the concept of "managed lanes," defined as "highway facilities or a set of lanes where operational strategies are proactively implemented and managed in response to changing conditions."

In expansion projects, it is important to consider cooperation across agencies and geographical borders as these projects frequently cross jurisdictional boundaries. Careful planning and project development is key to successful implementation.

As the system expands, equity may be a larger issue than when only one road was priced. Other equity considerations, such as rural and urban issues, should be addressed as well as the market and societal equity at either end or either side of the project boundaries.

**Tolling Expansion**

For the purposes of this guidebook, we will think in terms of a city planning to expand tolling along its roadway network as follows: city Y currently accessible from three directions: north, south, and east. The north Interstate currently has an HOT lane while the south Interstate only has general purpose lanes. The east access road is a highway corridor with an adjacent arterial, also un-priced. Due to current budget shortfalls, funding is insufficient to add general purpose lanes to the south Interstate and east highways. Thus, expanding the HOT network to these facilities, utilizing their existing footprints, is now being considered.

# 3.0. Congestion Pricing Equity - Definition and Factors

Section 3.0 provides a comprehensive definition of congestion and road pricing equity and describes the elements or factors that should be considered when evaluating the impacts of road pricing projects on communities and transportation system users.

## 3.1. Definition of Types of Equity

In simplest terms, equity means treating people of all social groups equally. In order for this definition to be meaningful, a definition of the following characteristics is needed:

- What constitutes equal treatment (called equity type), and
- Which social groupings are being observed (called equity category or unit of analysis).

Because equity is a very broad topic, the scope of equity being discussed should be limited. In addition to equity type and the category or unit of analysis, two further characteristics must be identified: impacts of concern and measures to assess equity impact. Impacts of concern are the aspects of the lives of travelers that are affected by the transportation or pricing project. Typical categories of impacts that are relevant to transportation equity include financial/economic, transportation service, or environmental impacts. Sometimes these impacts of concern are referred to as "social exclusions," which means the transportation system by either price, area of service, or vehicle category is perceived to be biased against a social class, poor neighborhood, or beyond the financial reach of a percentage of the population; for example, a new highway that does not have an interchange at or near the lower income housing area of the urban center. Another example is an electric vehicle that does not pay any fuel taxes but is priced sufficiently high that only the upper economic classes can afford to buy one. This latter example is a new concern as high efficiency and alternate fuel vehicles start entering the overall vehicle fleet.

In order to compare the equity discussions from one project to another, the impacts must be measured in units that allow comparison across projects of different size, passenger utilization, etc. Such measures may be per capita, per vehicle mile, per trip, etc. In terms of "social inequities," for example, the measure to assess equity impacts between an electric vehicle and carbon-based fuel vehicle could be translated to the dollar value of tax paid by one versus the other. Alternatively, one could translate it to the amount of lane miles driven per refill to show the social inequity of a plug-in hybrid versus vehicle versus a conventional carbon-based fuel vehicle. In either example, the measures of comparison must be comparative to show the degree of social inequity of one case versus another.

Economists and social theorists have defined several types of equity that can be applied to transportation projects. At the highest level, the categories are horizontal equity and vertical equity. Every system can be defined in terms of horizontal social equity and vertical equity at any point along the horizontal axis. Typically, social inequity is a horizontal measure while social exclusion is a vertical equity argument.

***Horizontal Equity***

Horizontal equity, also called fairness and egalitarianism, defines equity as the equal distribution of impacts (costs and benefits) between distinct individuals and groups that are considered equal in ability or need. Horizontal equity means that each group of the same class is treated the same. Horizontal equity makes no claim whatsoever about distribution between different classes. Horizontal equity generally falls into two categories: opportunity equity and market equity. Agencies often achieve horizontal equity by applying principals of both.

**Opportunity Equity**

Opportunity equity requires that costs and benefits are assigned in proportion to the size of the group without regard to any other group characteristics. In the case of road pricing, opportunity equity means that the costs and benefits of a new transportation project should be divided proportionately among social groups. An example of opportunity equity in road pricing is with respect to geography: each individual pays the same rate regardless of starting point. This means that one-way tolls, such as are used on some bridges in the Northeast, do not exhibit full horizontal equity (though many people using these bridges make round-trips and thus pay an equal toll, there is a small population who do not and thus are exposed to horizontally inequity). Opportunity equity is a type of horizontal equity because it does not consider the resources, socio-economic class, etc., of individuals.

**Market Equity**

Market equity in road pricing is achieved when the price charged to each individual or group is in direct proportion to the costs imposed and the benefits received by the individual or group. An example of market equity in road pricing would be setting a congestion charge for a driver entering a congested area at a specific time to correspond precisely to the cost of the induced delay the driver imposed upon other drivers—as the amount of imposed delay would vary by the level of congestion, the price would correspondingly vary. Market equity is a type of horizontal equity because it does not consider the resources, class, etc., of individuals—everyone pays the same market-based rate.

***Vertical Equity or Outcome Equity***

Vertical or outcome equity refers to the distribution of impacts (costs and benefits) across social groups that differ in ability and/or need. The principle of vertical equity is that individuals with less ability and/or more need should bear less of the cost and/or accrue more of the benefits of a project, and conversely, that individuals with more ability and/or less need should bear more of the cost and/or accrue more of the benefits of the project. The minimum statement of vertical equity is that the worst off should be made no worse off. Social groupings used in vertical equity include income or social class, or with respect to mobility need and ability. In road pricing projects, a type of vertical equity with respect to income is achieved by noting that lower income individuals are more likely to use buses or other forms of public transportation. Thus when a flat road charge is imposed by an agency creating more vertical inequity (because the lower income individuals pay a higher percentage of their income for the charge than higher income individuals), the inequity can be mitigated by increasing public transportation service to, from, and within the area subject to the road charge.

***Additional Types of Equity***

- **Spatial Equity** - The extent to which benefits and costs are distributed equally over space.
- **Intergenerational Equity** - The extent to which benefits and losses/costs are distributed to the present or the future.
- **Social Equity** - The extent to which allocation is proportionate to need.
- **Operational Equity** - The extent to which benefits and costs are distributed among system users for different operational strategies. With the greater prevalence of dynamic pricing that varies with congestion, the same facility may have prices that vary from day to day in addition to time of day. Thus, a trip at 7:30 a.m. may be priced differently on Monday than it is on Wednesday or even on Monday of the previous week.

**Table 3-1. Taxonomy of Transportation Equity**

| Type | Subtype | Description |
|---|---|---|
| Horizontal | Opportunity | Groups/individuals of the same ability/need are given costs/benefits in proportion to their size |
| | Market | Groups/individuals of the same ability/need are charged a cost in proportion to benefits received |
| Vertical/ Outcome | | Groups/individuals of differing ability/need achieve the same result |

Horizontal, vertical, and spatial equities are often considered in road pricing projects. Spatial equity is often cited as a key reason for expanding a toll network to adjacent regions to allow a larger population to benefit from additional travel options, including priced lanes with faster travel times and/or new transit service. Interregional equity is a priority when an agency is considering long-term lease agreements with private companies and may receive a lump-sum payment now, but toll users will pay far into the future. Market, social, and operational equity are addressed or accounted for less often.

These different types of equity often overlap and conflict. For example, horizontal equity requires that users bear the costs of their transportation facilities and services, but vertical equity often requires subsidies for disadvantaged people. Transportation planning often involves making tradeoffs between different equity objectives. State and local government officials will want to understand equity considerations so that they can explain the equity issues to the public on a given road pricing project.

## 3.2. Equity Units of Analysis

The primary scope of an equity measurement is its category or unit of analysis, the grouping of individuals for whom equity is analyzed. Typical units of analysis for equity include geographic, stakeholder groups, and individuals. Of these units, stakeholder groups are among the most commonly analyzed in transportation equity literature. This section will provide some examples of different types of stakeholder groups as applied to the above types of equity. The guidebook will be used by state and local governments so the team will highlight state and local governments as a stakeholder group, separately from other groups such as the American Highway Users Alliance or other advocate groups.

For horizontal equity analysis, stakeholder groups may be ethnic groups, groups who primarily use one mode of transportation (transit, passenger vehicle, walk/bike), or other groups. A new type of horizontal equity concerns infrastructure payment by various stakeholder groups. This focuses on equity of each class of user of the mobility network paying their own share for the use of the network infrastructure. Payment for infrastructure has long been based on the ubiquitous use of fuel taxes paid into a dedicated (hypothecated) fund (the Highway Trust Fund). The advance of electric, plug-in hybrids, high-efficiency petroleum, and hydrogen fuel vehicles has created new classes of road users. These new classes are not buying fuel and paying proportionate taxes to support the infrastructure they use. Drivers of fully electric vehicles such as the Tesla Roadster and the Nissan Leaf (which sold out its first year model run of 20,000 vehicles) are paying no fuel tax towards highway infrastructure whatsoever. From the perspective of horizontal equity with respect to infrastructure payment, this situation is not equitable, though it may encourage adoption of the use of lower emissions vehicles.

Vertical equity is commonly measured with respect to stakeholders grouped by income or social class: lower income classes should bear less of the cost and/or accrue more of the benefits than upper income classes. An alternative application of vertical equity is achieved by grouping stakeholders according to mobility need and ability. This application says in essence that those who have greatest need for mobility and/or are least capable of accessing transportation should accrue the most benefits and/or pay the least costs for a transportation project. By grouping stakeholders according to mobility need and ability, equity measures the degree to which the transportation system meets the needs of travelers with special constraints and is frequently invoked to justify paratransit services.

**Payment Medium Access Equity**

One significant stakeholder group affected by road pricing projects are "unbanked" people—people who have no bank accounts, by choice or because they lack the financial means. Some agencies require that users have bank accounts in order to obtain the means to pay the fare on a given road pricing project. Yet the number of unbanked people remains as high as 10-20 percent in many places, and denying these people access to priced road projects can significantly harm equity.[4] Those tolling projects require users to have transponders, thus preventing the legal usage of the facility by a significant portion of the population, a situation that would be considered inequitable by both vertical and horizontal measures. Many other facilities also allow users to pay video tolling fees (a camera reads the license plate and the owner is billed by mail), which are slightly higher than the EZ-Pass fees, to account for additional costs of processing. While this arrangement allows unbanked individuals to use the project legally, it requires them to pay more than others, which is also inequitable by standard vertical and horizontal measures. Measures to mitigate this equity issue include providing transponders to drivers using cash, and providing cash "top up" stations(kiosks that allow account holders to pay cash to increase their balance) at supermarkets or gas stations; or simply allowing video tolling for the same price as transponder tolling—a measure sure to substantially increase operating costs due to the inherent inefficiencies in video tolling. Maryland's Intercounty Connector is one of several road pricing facilities in the United States that allows payments with an EZ-Pass, which requires users to have either a bank account or to pay by cash.

## 3.3. Definitions of "Impacts of Concern" by Equity Type and Analysis Unit

"Impacts of concern" refer to the changes in the lives of the traveling public (as divided according to the categories or units of analysis) caused by the transportation project for which equity implications will be observed. There are three main groups of impacts of concern that are observed for road pricing projects:

- *Financial and economic user costs and benefits*: this group of impacts includes the direct financial and economic costs and benefits of the transportation project to both users of the system and those living in the region affected by the system. User financial costs include direct financial costs (charges) and indirect financial costs (transponder rental, banking costs, costs incurred changing routes or times to avoid the charges). Non-user financial costs may include upfront costs for implementing the system (typically taken from general funds). Financial and economic benefits experienced by both users and non-users include overall greater economic productivity and growth due to more efficient use of the transportation system.
- *Transportation system impacts:* user transportation benefits may include increased service quality, travel time reductions (decrease in congestion or delays), or increase in trip time reliability. These benefits may be experienced not only by road system users but also by transit users in systems where transit receives funding from road revenues or where transit services utilize the road pricing system (e.g., buses through the tolled region). Transportation harms may include extra traffic on areas bordering pricing regions.
- *External impacts*: this group includes the impacts that the transportation activity has on all individuals external to the transportation transaction. Specific external impacts may include environmental impacts (such as net CO2 emissions, or emissions of

polluting gases such as NOx), safety impacts (increases or decreases in road safety), and congestion/delay impacts (road delay or congestion caused by traveling).

Non-users are potentially important in terms of equity impacts. Affected non-users include travelers using adjacent non-priced facilities, residents and business owners along the priced facility, residents and business owners on the adjacent facilities, existing transit riders that may be affected by a larger number of transit riders and improved transit service, etc. User costs and benefits will include pre- pricing-implementation users of the road that benefit from a road pricing project and pre-pricing users that may accrue non-benefits (detrimental costs) from a road-pricing project and thus may not be able to continue to use the road at their preferred times.

## 3.4. Definitions of Measures to Assess Potential Equity Impact

The size, scope, and average daily traffic on pricing facilities vary widely. To allow for comparison between projects or between the present situation and the future situation (after the project is built), the equity impacts must employ measures that account for the size of the project. There are several measures to assess equity impacts that allow for comparisons, including the following:

- *Per capita*: what are the impacts per person using the pricing project? This can further be refined by specific groups: per adult, per commuter, per household, etc. Per capita measures treat all passengers equally, whether they are driving single-occupancy vehicles or riding in large transit vehicles.
- *Per vehicle mile*: what are the impacts per vehicle mile traveled by any vehicle in the pricing project? This can further be refined by specifying the type of roadway (per highway mile, per arterial mile) and/or the type of vehicle (per bus mile, per car mile). Per vehicle mile measures treat all vehicles equally, regardless of occupancy.
- *Per trip*: what are the impacts per trip taken? This measure is not the same as per capita, because travelers do not always take the same number of trips per week: some may take 2 per day, while some may take many more. This can be further refined by specifying the purpose or time of the trip: per commute trip, per peak-period trip, etc. Like

per capita, per trip measures treat all passengers equally, regardless of their mode or vehicle.

- *Per dollar*: what are the impacts of the program per dollar paid for the charge? This can be further refined by specifying the type of expenditure: dollar of user fee paid, dollar of tax paid.

Table 3-2 summarizes the main possibilities of the four characteristics that define equity.

## 3.5. State and Local Consideration for Equity Type, Category, Impacts of Concern, and Measures

During the initial phase of project evaluation, agencies should develop a plan to identify the equity factors that should be considered when assessing the impacts of road pricing strategies. As demonstrated in Table 3-2, for each road pricing strategy agencies should answer the following questions:

- What types of potential equity impacts should be evaluated for the proposed road pricing strategy?

**Table 3-2. Indicative List of the four Characteristics that Define Equity[5]**

| Types of Equity | Categories/ Units of Analysis | Impacts of Concern | Measures to Assess Equity Impact |
|---|---|---|---|
| **Horizontal**<br>Opportunity<br>Market<br>**Vertical/ Outcome** | Income<br>Geographic (location)<br>Demographic (race, gender, etc.)<br>Ability<br>Mode<br>Vehicle type<br>Trip Type | **Financial / Economic**<br>Price/Fare structure<br>Economic opportunity & development<br>Other Financial/ Economic<br>**Transportation Service**<br>Delay Reliability<br>Other service quality metrics<br>**External**<br>Crash risk<br>Induced congestion<br>Emissions<br>Noise | Per Capita<br>Per Trip<br>Per vehicle mile<br>Per Dollar |

- What are the equity categories most likely affected by the proposed pricing strategy?
- What are the likely qualitative and quantitative impacts that would result should the proposed congestion strategy be implemented?
- What measurement units should agencies use to best measure the costs and benefits of the proposed congestion strategy?

The process of incorporating equity analysis into the transportation planning process and the methods to evaluate the impacts of congestion and road pricing strategies are discussed further in Sections 4 and 5.

## Scenario 1: Agencies Considering Implementing Roadway Congestion Pricing Strategies for the First Time

State, regional, and/or local agencies should consider how groups with different incomes are impacted by high occupancy toll (HOT) lanes. HOT lanes are considered relatively equitable since a free alternative is adjacent to the tolled alternative. As an example of equity classification and evaluation, transportation agencies should evaluate the travel time differences of drivers of all incomes and races between taking the tolled lane vs. the adjacent free lanes. This way they can consider what income proportion is used when paying the toll and for how much travel time savings.

## Scenario 2: Agencies Considering Road Pricing Expansion along Their Network

State, regional, and local agencies considering expanding an existing toll system should account for the entire network effects of expanding their system. Now that multiple roads are under consideration for tolling, potential geographic impacts, market and societal equity come into play.
It may be that drivers from certain communities now have fewer un-priced choices. Evaluation may include estimating tolls by minute of travel time savings offset by additional transit service using the faster tolled lanes.

### 3.6. Classification of Equity in Congestion and Road Pricing Initiatives – Illustrative Examples

As discussed earlier, the two scenarios identified in Section 2.0 are used in the remaining sections of this report to help demonstrate new concepts and guidelines. These scenarios are intended to be illustrative rather than comprehensive. Each scenario will likely need to address multiple types of equity.

## 4.0. INCORPORATING EQUITY IN THE TRANSPORTATION PLANNING PROCESS

Equity analysis will be most effective if it is incorporated into the development of road pricing projects from the beginning. This is especially true of the design of the pricing structure, where failure to address equity concerns may necessitate a complete reanalysis.

### 4.1. General Guidelines to Consider when Incorporating Equity in the Transportation Planning Process

There are some general guidelines that all public agencies contemplating road pricing projects should follow in order to measure and evaluate equity impacts. It is likely that the same agency or group of agencies that is proposing a project will be responsible for all aspects of the project, including evaluation, implementing potential remediation schemes, and communicating about the project. In theory, the evaluation and its results should be independent from the entity performing the evaluation, be it a State or a local department of transportation, a Metropolitan Planning Organization, or any other planning authority. In practice, these agencies may need to participate in the evaluation as they may control the revenue generated. When this is the case, all of the participating agencies should be involved and the process should be open and transparent. All agencies should try to follow guidelines and procedures consistent with those listed in Table 4-1.

1. **Consider equity impacts early and throughout the project planning process:** Agencies will benefit from identifying and

measuring potential equity impacts early and throughout the process, which should lead to greater awareness and public acceptance and ultimately success of the road pricing project.

2. **Determine users potentially impacted by the proposed project as well as regional equity priorities:** Section 3.0 demonstrated that various categories of users may become impacted by a particular road pricing project. How the impacts are measured may vary with whether the proposed road pricing project impacts low income travelers, particular ethnic groups, particular residents, and/or travelers with less access to alternative travel modes. A socio-economic analysis of an agency's and a project's regional boundaries can help identify the various demographic, socioeconomic, industry, and other system user groups potentially affected by the proposed road pricing initiative. Evaluating and measuring the impacts of congestion pricing strategies on system users is discussed in more detail in Section 5.0. The magnitude of road pricing equity impacts will likely influence the choice of an appropriate remediation method (addressed in Section 6).
3. **Evaluate equity impacts of the base case or "no build" alternative as well as the impact of the road pricing project:** A roadway may have a negative impact on low-income travelers or particular residents with less access to alternative modes whether or not the roadway is priced. A limited access roadway (such as a highway) may limit local connectivity and access to shopping and services. There may be externalities like noise and air pollution. For these reasons and others it is important to consider impacts of the no-build scenario as well as the impact of the road pricing project. Part of the baseline evaluation is that, at a minimum, an agency should "do no additional harm" with a road pricing project.
4. **Consider a variety of perspectives and impacts:** It is likely that all projects will have groups of people that benefit from the project and may have other groups that are negatively affected. Project evaluation should consider impacts on all impacted groups, not just those on lower income people or the residents of one particular neighborhood. It is better to consider multiple origins and destinations and multiple types of potential users.
5. **Measure effects:** Section 5.0 describes several qualitative and quantitative methodologies for measuring equity impacts. Until impacts are quantified and compared against the base, no-build case,

it is difficult to fully understand how the project affects different groups.

**Table 4-1. Equity Evaluation Guidelines**

| |
|---|
| Step1. Consider any potential equity impacts of pricing early in the project—during the planning and design phases. |
| Step 2. Determine who may potentially be impacted by the project. What kind of equity is important? |
| Step 3. Evaluate potential equity impacts of the base case or "no build" alternative to compare against the equity impact of the road pricing project. |
| Step 4. Consider variety of perspectives and impacts. |
| Step 5. Measure effects (measuring equity impacts is addressed in Section 5). |

**Table 4-2. Procedure for Conducting an Environmental Justice Analysis**[6]

| |
|---|
| **Scoping**<br>• Clearly identify the composition of the region of influence and include appropriate criteria and data on the community.<br>• Analyze the identification of the region of influence using appropriate data on the affected community.<br>• Ensure that the affected community input during the scoping process includes access to information and meetings. |
| **Affected Area and Composition of Region of Influence**<br>• Define the criteria for recognizing the affected community and do criteria include minority and low-income groups and Indian tribes.<br>• Analyze the affected community and include information on patterns of subsistence consumption of fish, vegetation, or wildlife.<br>• Ensure that the community provides input to the identification of the community of concern and has associated access to information and meetings. |
| **Identify Sources of Exposure**<br>• Identify the sources of exposure and likelihood of exposure to the affected community including potential environmental, human health, social, economic, and cultural impacts.<br>• Analyze potential direct, indirect, multiple, and cumulative impacts to the affected community. |

- Ensure that the affected community's input is considered in the identification of the sources of exposure and likelihood of exposure. Also that they receive access to information and meetings.

**Potential for Disproportionate Effects**

- Identify the potential or adverse impacts on the community and whether they include potential environmental, human health, social, economic, and cultural impacts.
- Analyze the potential for adverse impacts and evaluate both whether it is disproportionate on the community and whether it includes potential environmental, human health, social, economic, and cultural impacts.
- Ensure that community provides input in the assessment of impacts and potential for disproportionate impacts on the community and has access to information and meetings.

**Determine Actions**

- Identify potential alternatives, mitigation measures, and monitoring to minimize the potential impact on the community.
- Analyze the potential alternatives, mitigation measures, and monitoring to minimize the potential impact to the community.
- Ensure community input to the identification of actions and ensure access to information and meetings.

## 4.2. An Example of Equity Analysis: Environmental Justice

Environmental Justice (EJ) is a type of equity in which only environmental impacts are considered. Because equity analysis encompasses more than just an environmental justice analysis, this guidebook recommends that agencies perform a larger equity analysis as they contemplate road pricing projects and implement road pricing. The equity analysis should be performed in addition to any environmental evaluation required by law.

As described in Table 4-2, procedures for an EJ analysis illustrate how equity analysis can be completed. EJ Analysis is a type of equity analysis that focuses on environmental impacts. The guideline provided in Table 4-2 is based on actual analysis performed on Environmental Protection Agency (EPA) projects where 200 draft Environmental Impact statements were reviewed to determine how many EJ analyses were performed as part of the Environmental Impact Statement process. The project analyzed EJ impacts related to project scope, affected project area, sources of exposure, potential for disproportionate effects, and project actions. The emphasis is not just on potential impacts of project alternatives on the affected community, but whether the community participated in project inputs and project meetings.

FHWA and the Texas Department of Transportation (TxDOT) compiled detailed how-to guidance in April 2009 for how to perform project-level and network-level environmental justice evaluations of toll roads. In this case, ***this is the equivalent to what can be done for a road pricing equity analysis***. The document explains that an EJ area may be one where minorities or low-income populations in the traffic analysis zone (TAZ) exceed 50 percent. The general guidance is presented in Table 4-3.

The FHWA/TxDOT source also describes evaluation of a network of toll roads which includes priced managed lanes.[8] In addition to the information highlighted in Table 4-3, the source includes how the network will be tolled over time, an estimation of the cumulative economic impact of the tolls and expanding toll network, and a comparison of the tolled and non-tolled network benefits over time.

**Table 4-3. Project-Level Evaluation of Toll Roads[7]**

***All projects should document and discuss:***

- Available non-tolled facilities (that can be used as substitutes for the tolled facility).
- Travel time differences between tolled and non-tolled routes.
- Transit vehicle toll policies.
- Toll rates or toll ranges.
- Methods of toll collection and how they may affect access and cost.
- Cost differences between acquiring toll tag with credit card or with cash.
- Location of toll booths, particularly in relation to identified EJ areas.
- EJ-related demographic data by traffic analysis zone (TAZ).
- Potential economic impact to individuals (for example, assuming 250 tolled round trips to work per year) and calculating toll proportion of income.
- Expected use of toll revenues.
- Potential remediation measures.
- Accommodations for Limited English Proficiency and disabled travelers to use the toll facility.
- Potential users of the facility using origin and destination studies identified by decreased travel time with use of the tolled facility.
- Assumptions and limitations of any travel demand models used in the study.

## 4.3. Incorporating Equity in the Transportation Planning Process – Illustrative Examples

To further illustrate how agencies should consider equity in evaluating their projects, each of the scenarios described in Section 2.0 is presented below along with a discussion around how equity should be incorporated in each scenario.

### SCENARIO 1: AGENCIES CONSIDERING IMPLEMENTING ROADWAY CONGESTION PRICING STRATEGIES FOR THE FIRST TIME

County X should consider equity impacts early and often in contemplating their potential pricing project. Transportation planners and decisionmakers should consider users impacted by the proposed tolling strategy. Since they are considering tolling an HOV lane adjacent to non-tolled lanes, then they already have identified a substitutable non-tolled lane. As such, county X's equity analysis should focus primarily on the tolled lane potential users, specifically how the tolled travel time compares to the travel time on the non-tolled lanes and how toll fares are collected.

### SCENARIO 2: AGENCIES CONSIDERING ROAD PRICING EXPANSION ALONG THEIR NETWORK

City Y should consider the network effects of their expanding system. And equity issues did not arise before when only one road was tolled, but now that several roads are likely to be tolled and the additional roads do not have existing HOV or HOT lanes, road pricing equity impacts could be substantial. The public often balks at charges for roadways that had previously been un-tolled. If the pricing expansion ensures that all priced lanes also accommodate HOV for free, then the equity impacts may be reduced. Transportation planners and decisionmakers in city Y should identify potential equity impacts early on rather than continue to ignore equity considerations. Without considering equity and user impacts early, there may be concerns about the city's ability to successfully implement its toll expansion initiative.

# 5.0. EVALUATING EQUITY AT THE PROJECT LEVEL

The equity measurement procedures and methods described in Section 5.0 can be used by agencies at all levels of government (State, regional, and local). Proactive agencies consider equity impacts at project initiation and become aware of potential and actual project impacts as part of project planning. In contrast, reactive agencies consider equity impacts after concerns are raised by stakeholders that the project has negative equity impacts and that equity should be addressed. Both proactive and reactive agencies should determine who is affected and measure potential impacts. Both will adopt the same evaluation methodologies to their projects. The illustrative scenarios presented at the end of Section 5.0 provide examples of how an agency approaches equity evaluation proactively or reactively.

## 5.1. Procedure for Evaluating Equity at the Project Level

Agencies may find it helpful to evaluate the equity impacts of pricing projects on an ongoing basis during the design of the project. To evaluate equity impacts of any road pricing project, the first step is to define the specific kinds of equity (Section 3.0) that should be analyzed: the unique combinations of the four characteristics described previously.

The following procedure is a starting point for agencies desiring to assess equity impacts:

- Determine the stakeholder groups that could potentially be affected by a given project.
- Catalog the known concerns of the major stakeholder groups that will be affected, and make best guesses as to which kinds of equity will matter to them. Choose only the top few kinds for each stakeholder group.
- Internally, use modeling to determine impacts on the types of equity chosen for analysis. Modeling techniques may include the following:
  - Transportation modeling
  - Financial modeling
  - Environmental modeling.
- Design mitigation strategies (such as those described in Section 6) to mitigate significant equity impacts.

- Hold stakeholder outreach meetings to explain the project. Explain how the project creates a net social benefit, and explain the mitigation strategies to those who would perceive harm. After the stakeholders understand the system, ask for their remaining concerns about the project. Stakeholders should be engaged early in the process, but not before the first efforts at alleviating equity concerns are incorporated into the project design.
- Based on stakeholder concerns from the meeting, consider whether further mitigation strategies are warranted.
- Continue to work with stakeholder groups throughout project implementation to ensure that no new equity concerns arise.

## 5.2. Evaluating the Impacts of Road Pricing Projects – Qualitative and Quantitative Techniques

There seems to be little consensus among experts on what methodologies to use to measure the cost and benefits of road pricing initiatives. Appropriate evaluation methodologies can vary based upon the specific equity measure desired, data availability, and agency staff expertise in conducting equity analyses for road pricing projects. This guidebook provides instructions to help standardize processes for all State and local agencies to use in evaluating equity.

Evaluation methodologies can be categorized as qualitative or quantitative. Qualitative evaluation methods can be used as an initial step towards quantitative evaluation, but quantitative measures should be used to measure actual impacts. The following text provides brief summaries of several potential evaluation methods.

### *Identification of Beneficiaries and Those Potentially Negatively Impacted – Qualitative Evaluation*

Table 5-1 provides example road pricing beneficiaries and those potentially negatively impacted. As shown, an initial catalog of who directly benefits or dis-benefits (i.e., receives harm) from a road pricing project helps to illustrate project impacts. Once these are identified, a quantitative analysis of the size of the benefits and dis-benefits can be made. A general agency goal, beyond "do no additional harm" is that the aggregated benefits of a project outweigh the aggregated dis-benefits.

**Table 5-1. Example Road Pricing Beneficiaries and Those Potentially Negatively Impacted**

| Direct Beneficiaries | Potentially Negatively Impacted |
|---|---|
| • Wealthier motorists who value their travel time savings more than their toll costs<br>• Bus and rideshare travelers who enjoy improved service due to reduced congestion and economies of scale<br>• Recipients of toll revenues<br>• Local and regional communities who enjoy a better quality of life, less noise pollution, and emissions | • Lower income motorists who pay the toll because they have no travel alternative, but don't value their time savings more than the toll costs<br>• Motorists who shift to other routes to avoid a toll<br>• Road users on un-tolled roads who experience increased congestion<br>• Motorists who forego trips due to tolls<br>• Motorists who shift to transit and rideshare modes due to tolls (although service improvements due to economies of scale may make some of these net beneficiaries) |

Note: Contents adapted from original.

Source: Gomez-Ibanez, Jose, "The Political Economy of Highway Tolls and Congestion Pricing," Journal of Transport Economics and Policy, Vol. 46, No. 3, July 1992, pp. 343-360. Repeated in Litman, Todd, "Using Road Pricing Revenue: Economic Efficiency and Equity Considerations," May 2011. Found at http://www.vtpi.org/revenue.pdf. Accessed January 18, 2012

### *Before and after Road Pricing Equity Impacts*

A simpler way to measure equity impacts is to measure equity impacts before a road pricing scheme is implemented and then to measure the impacts after a scheme is implemented. As with all evaluation, there are advantages to measuring the actual project implementation and impacts, but there may be reasons why we want to predict the impact of projects that are only in the planning stages. For the scientifically rigorous before-and-after and cross-sectional studies to measure the equity implications of evolving financing mechanisms in order to provide a robust basis for future decisionmaking, the report states that the studies should:

- Track short- and long-term behavioral shifts in response to the evolving mechanisms
- Conduct verifiable analyses to ensure the validity and transferability of results
- Avoid preconceived notions and oversimplification.[9]

### *Direct and Indirect Road Pricing Cost and Benefit Calculations*

Weinstein and Sciara suggest considering both direct and indirect cost and benefit calculations in evaluating the equity of road pricing projects. [10] They suggest that tolls are regressive but that there are many socially acceptable government fees like garbage collection fees, community college tuition, and fees to use public swimming pools. They suggest considering the evidence from existing HOT lanes that some low-income people do use the lanes indicating that they feel the benefits are greater than the cost of the toll. Many priced managed lane users are only occasional users—for certain occasions the toll is a price that most people can afford. They suggest the following indirect benefits—that the reallocation of revenues to enhance transit or match carpools or provide other transportation services may provide all corridor users including lower income travelers with enhanced and faster transportation options. Another benefit suggested earlier in the guidebook is that some HOT lanes have reduced the travel times on the general purpose lanes, providing a benefit to all corridor users. Weinstein and Sciara finally suggest that the benefit and cost calculations also need to consider indirect costs like transponder deposits and acquisition.

### *GIS Analysis of Who is Affected by a Road Pricing Project*

The FHWA/TxDOT paper referred to in Section 4.0 suggests using Geographical Information Systems (GIS) to determine which residential areas may benefit from the faster travel times of a road pricing project.[11] As described earlier, the travel times from each regional neighborhood to typical destinations using the priced and substitutable unpriced roadways should be calculated to determine the potential benefits and impacts of the priced facility. GIS may also help identify which residential areas are adjacent to a road pricing project and which areas may have increased noise from the faster traveling vehicles on a priced roadway. These noise-related dis-benefits may be offset by the air quality reductions resulting from faster moving vehicles.

### *Econometric Analysis with Survey Data*

One way to quantitatively assess the impacts of a road pricing project is to obtain both demographic and travel behavior data of potential and actual project users. An econometric analysis can then be performed to determine which variables contribute to the choice of using a priced lane. Econometric analyses may also be used to determine the frequency of using a priced option. Demographics include income, gender, vehicle ownership rates, and household size. Travel behavior includes origin and destination at a minimum, but may also include attitudes towards pricing and how travel times, travel time reliability, number of signals, and type of roadway impact route choice decisions.

A number of papers in the literature perform econometric analyses related to road pricing, but the ones that specifically address equity are limited. A recent project at the University of Washington used non- project-specific regional data for their analysis including the 2007 American Community Survey, the Washington Population Survey for 2004 and 2006, and the Puget Sound Regional Council's 2006 Household Activities Survey. The paper found that the ACS provided the best demographic data but they needed to integrate the ACS data with the Household Activity survey data for travel routes of poor and non-poor households.[12] The researchers used the data to determine the percentage of income used in paying tolls for two different scenarios: a network of tolled roadways and one priced bridge (SR 520 which initiated tolls in December 2011).

Burris and Hannay performed the more-common analysis of acquiring demographic and travel behavior data from project-specific survey data; in this case, a survey of Houston QuickRide enrollees.[13] The analyses determined that priced roadway usage did not vary significantly by income, occupation, age, or household size. Similarly, frequency of usage did not vary significantly; however, QuickRide enrollees were found to have significantly higher incomes and were significantly younger than drivers on the adjacent general purpose lanes. Burris and Hannay suggest that the ability or interest of low-income individuals to enroll in the program is an equity concern but that as long as the occupants of the QuickRide program valued their time at more than $3 an hour, the program had a net benefit.

### *Road Pricing versus Alternative Non-Tolled Projects and Remediation Strategies*

In addition to the proposed road pricing project, alternative projects should be identified. An understanding of the base conditions without the road pricing project is also needed. After this step, the agency can start measuring the additional benefits or dis-benefits of the road pricing project compared to not implementing the road pricing project. It may be, for example, that certain geographic areas are adversely affected by a roadway whether or not the roadway is tolled.

As the groups that are affected are identified, remediation strategies should be considered for addressing potential equity impacts. Several of these remediation strategies including toll design, toll discounts, and revenue redistribution are presented in Section 6.0.

## 5.3. Evaluating Equity at the Project Level – Illustrative Examples

For each of the two scenarios described in Section 2.0, an illustrative example of how to evaluate the equity impact of a pricing project is offered below.

| **Scenario 1: Agencies Considering Implementing Roadway Congestion Pricing Strategies for the First Time** | |
|---|---|
| **Potential Evaluation Method** | • **Direct and Indirect Cost and Benefit Calculation** |
| **Description:** The tolling agency in county X should attempt to calculate direct and indirect costs and benefits of potential users and non-users in the priced managed lane corridor. Direct costs include the expected tolls to be paid. Indirect costs include transponder acquisition and deposit, obtaining information about travel time differences between the priced and general purpose lanes. Direct benefits include travel time savings for both the priced managed lane users and general purpose lane users. Indirect benefits include not having to travel in a carpool to use the faster lane and improved air quality due to the higher speed of the general purpose lanes. | |

| **Scenario 2: Agencies Considering Road Pricing Expansion along Their Network** | |
|---|---|
| **Potential Evaluation Method** | • **Econometric Analysis with Project-Specific Survey** |
| **Description:** With the experience of priced managed lanes in the region, the tolling agency in city Y can survey users (both priced managed lane users and general purpose lane users) of the corridor and the proposed toll corridors. The survey can result in demographic data including income, household size, occupation, age and gender and travel behavior data of typical origin, typical destination, priced managed lane HOT lane usage frequency, commuting frequency, and attitudes about priced managed lanes and pricing. With this data, the agency can determine what factors impact priced managed lane usage frequency and assess how the expanded tolled roadways may be utilized. | |

# 6.0. Strategies to Address and Mitigate the Impacts of Congestion Pricing

Section 6.0 offers transportation planners and decisionmakers procedures and guidelines to help address and mitigate the equity impacts of road pricing strategies.

## 6.1. Congestion Pricing Remediation Strategies in the Literature

Some earlier papers suggest how revenues gained from road pricing projects should be redistributed to make road pricing more politically viable. Goodwin suggests a "Rule of Three" and distributing revenues to tax relief, new roads, and public transportation.[14] Small provides seven recommendations for how revenue should be utilized.[15] But neither of these emphasize that this revenue distribution is to remediate adverse equity impacts; the larger emphasis is road pricing viability. In contrast to these and similar, earlier papers, the emphasis of Section 6.0 is remediation in response to equity impacts.

TRB Special Report 303[16] cautions that there may be limited funding for remediation measures, especially if the road pricing revenues go to further road construction or debt service. Another report suggests that remediation measures should be assessed by whether they treat everyone equally, whether people bear the costs that they impose, whether they are progressive with respect to income, whether they benefit the transportation disadvantaged, and whether they improve basic access.[17] Also, related to Section 7.0 on communications, stakeholders should be involved early in the process to help identify and target remedies.[18]

This section lists many different measures that can be used to remediate negative equity impacts of road pricing projects. There are a number of measures that agencies may employ to mitigate equity effects. These include:

- *Use of revenues*—judicious use of revenues generated by a pricing project is the single most important way of mitigating equity effects. The European Union's Coordination of Urban Road User Charging Organizational Issues (CURACAO's) road pricing fact sheet reads: "Evidence suggests that the judicious use of hypothecated revenues is likely to achieve a greater improvement in equity than simply reducing the overall charge level." In order to ensure such judicious use, the agency should, foremost, hypothecate or ring-fence revenues from the project for use on transportation. Such uses may include public transportation, but also highway operations and improvements. If the pricing program replaces other taxation sources, the pricing program may increase equity by many measures: Taylor and Schweitzer suggest that using road pricing to finance highway construction, maintenance and operations and thus reducing sales tax, increases vertical equity.[19]

- *Vary pricing by time of day, type and location of road, vehicle type, etc.* – use of pricing that varies by location, road type, time of day, vehicle type, and other characteristics may mitigate some equity impacts of pricing projects.
- *Discounts/Exemptions*—discounts and exemptions—in essence, varying pricing by person type—are a way of mitigating some demographic equity effects. However, such discounts and exemptions often lead to a greater need for enforcement and high administrative costs, and so should be avoided unless no other means of equity mitigation exists.
- *Provide payment means for the unbanked*—in order to avoid creating a system where the unbanked are unable to easily participate in a pricing project, the agency should provide a means for them to pay by cash, such as top up terminals in gas stations or grocery stores.

Remediation strategies generally fall under one of three categories listed below:

- Revising existing finance pricing policies;
- Offering exemptions, discounts, subsidies, or rebates to parties adversely affected by the policy; or
- Offering or improving alternative transportation services.[20]

Table 6-1 provides a listing of potential equity impact remediation strategies. Please note that each of the remediation measures or strategies listed in Table 6-1 is described in further detail Appendix B along with example deployment sites, benefactors, why the strategy is used, additional details, and links to more information. Table 6-2 describes some of the state and local financial as well as technology policies and strategies that might offset the benefits of equity impact mitigation measures.

At the end of section 6.0, we offer illustrative examples of potential remediation measures for each of the scenarios identified in Section 2.0.

**Table 6-1. Remediation Measures to Offset Equity Impacts, and Policy Choices that Complicate Remediation Measures**

| Method | Brief Description | Deployment site Examples |
|---|---|---|
| *Revising existing finance policies* | | |
| Credit-based congestion pricing[21] | Credit-based system to redistribute revenue to individual drivers | FAST miles[22] |
| Price Design limitations | Upper limits on road pricing, limits on the number of priced crossings per period for cordon charges, allowances for unlimited use of priced facilities in certain periods (off-peak hours, holidays, weekends, etc.) [23] | Widely implemented |
| Increased access to transponders | Allow motorists to apply for and receive transponders at public assistance offices and other sites commonly used by low-income populations. This may include customer service centers | Auto Expreso System in Puerto Rico<br>TxTag in Texas[24]<br>SR 520 bridge customer service centers in Washington |
| Alternative payment options | Offer cash or pay-as-you-go options for motorists who do not have debit/credit cards | Widely implemented (turnpike ticket option, cash for fare card, etc.) |
| Compensating nonusers | Offering compensation (i.e., toll credits) to drivers choosing to use general-purpose lanes | (Proposed) FAIR lanes[25] |
| Geographic system design | Purposefully locating cordon boundaries, exits, etc., in order to maximize equity | London and Stockholm cordon boundaries |
| Park and ride facilities | Parking adjacent to project or express bus stops to increase carpooling and transit use | I-95 Express Lanes in Broward County, FL<br>I-15 Express Lanes in San Diego, CA |

| Method | Brief Description | Deployment site Examples |
|---|---|---|
| *Offering exemptions, discounts, subsidies, or rebates to parties adversely affected by the policy* | | |
| Discounts/exemptions | Discounts reduce the congestion charge paid; exemptions exclude certain persons or vehicles from payment. May have cost and enforcement consequences | Most priced managed lane facilities exempt transit and emergency vehicles L.A. Metro – Toll Credit Program for low income users including discount and monthly fee waiver |
| Subsidies | Use a portion of revenue to subsidize toll costs/costs of low-income commuters | Central Texas toll roads (Texas 130, Loop 1, Texas 45N),[26] Germany, and France allow taxpayers to deduct commuting expenses from their income tax liability[27] |
| *Offering or improving alternative transportation services* | | |
| Revenue redistribution | Redistribute revenues through public spending on specific transportation-related improvements (widely implemented strategy on many priced managed lanes) | I-15 in San Diego (funds to support express bus service)[28] Norwegian toll rings (funds to roadway/transit improvement)[29] |
| Increased access to alternative transit | Transit, vanpools, paratransit, or other options as alternatives in locations not served by transit | Widely implemented |

The selection of remediation measures depends primarily on project objectives and conditions. A project emphasizing congestion reduction may adopt different remediation measures from a project with a revenue maximization emphasis. Similarly, a project with significant Federal funding may make choices differently than a locally funded project. The Los Angeles Metro project has an explicit Toll Credit Program for low income users to receive a credit at program sign-up and a waiver of monthly account fees. The Stockholm congestion charge has succeeded because special accommodations and mitigating measures were made for certain groups who perceived inequities, including the residents of a specific area (Lidingo Island).

Many recently deployed projects include the enhancement of transit options that take advantage of the faster facility. Use of toll revenues to support improved transit service has been one of the most successful strategies at gaining support from lower income groups as it provides mobility options that best serve these communities. However, Manchester, U.K., did not succeed in implementation of its congestion pricing project in part because automobile drivers perceived that a disproportionate amount of the anticipated revenues would be going to support riders of other modes.

More details are provided in Section 6.3 and in Appendix B.

## 6.2. Post-Implementation Road Pricing Remediation Strategies — Equity Audit Tool

Ecola and Light suggest the use of an "equity audit tool" after implementing a road pricing project. They suggest continuously monitoring the road pricing project and its remediation measures and determining whether the measures successfully address equity differences. If equity concerns are not well enough addressed, then either the road pricing project or the remediation can be modified to better address equity.[30]

| **Scenario 1: Agencies Considering Implementing Roadway Congestion Pricing Strategies for the First Time** | |
|---|---|
| **Issue** | • **Lack of Internet Access/Stable Address to Receive Mail** |
| **Potential Remediation Method** | • **Increased access to transponders** |
| **Description:** County X has an underutilized HOV lane. Converting to a HOT lane gives all drivers the opportunity to take advantage of the fourth lane, but often pricing a lane that was previously untolled is met with resistance. One way to encourage use of the newly converted HOT/Express lane is to make the technology as accessible and visible as possible. Making transponders convenient by selling them at local gas stations, retailers, etc. and providing cash-based purchase options to accommodate the unbanked will encourage drivers to acquire one and then utilize the new HOT/Express lane. This addresses payment medium equity and that some users are not able to utilize accounts that require credit cards or internet access. | |

| Scenario 2: Agencies Considering Road Pricing Expansion along Their Network | |
|---|---|
| **Issue** | **• Pricing Variations (time of day; miles traveled, etc...)** |
| **Potential Remediation Method** | **• Discounts/exemptions** |
| **Description:** The expansion of the tolled roadway network near city Y may coincide with a more-complicated tolling structure. Instead of charging just one toll to use the HOT/Express lane (regardless of traffic levels), the toll may vary by time of day and by miles traveled. It may also be possible for certain groups of users to apply for transponders that facilitate a discount. A simpler system follows the Los Angeles Metro example and provides a credit at account sign up and monthly fee waiver to low-income households. | |

### 6.3. Road Pricing Remediation Strategies – Illustrative Examples

In the following, the research team presents a potential remediation approach for each of the three road pricing scenarios identified. It is important to note that examples below are for illustrative purposes only; additional remediation methods likely apply to each of these scenarios.

## 7.0. The Role of Communications in Congestion Pricing Initiatives

Public perception and understanding of equity considerations are critical components for many road pricing initiatives. Much of the literature and our discussions with stakeholders relate to the importance of communications with respect to potential equity impacts on any of these projects. Communications should happen early and often in the project planning process and throughout the process. The literature stresses the importance of perception, acknowledging that road pricing is often perceived as unfair (e.g., the use of the "Lexus Lanes" moniker), and that there are differences in popular and expert perspectives.[31]

Communications may take on several forms including press releases, public meetings, glossy brochures, web sites, and speaking points for customer service representatives and agency staff. Agencies will likely need to use a variety of these methods to reach a large number of potential roadway users and potentially negatively impacted people. With appropriate communications, some of the questions and concerns surrounding the road pricing project may be addressed. With positive communications, users and local groups may be convinced of the roadway's benefits and less concerned with possible dis-benefits.

Section 7.0, presents a summary of what to communicate (Table 7-1) and also a summary of communications methods (Table 7-2). It also revisits the two illustrative scenarios from Section 2.0 and provides examples of what they should communicate about their projects and examples of how they should communicate it. For each particular project, agencies should review the charts below.

Agencies should carefully consider each of the proposed items in Table 7-1 and whether these apply to their projects and should be incorporated into their communications messages and strategies. Agencies should then review Table 7-2 and determine which of the communications methods can be adopted into their own project communications plans.

**Table 7-1. Selecting Equity-Related Messages to Communicate**

| What to Communicate | |
|---|---|
| **Description** | **Example** |
| Determining where and how revenues are used and how revenues will benefit roadway users | |
| Demonstrating benefits through experimental programs and pilot strategies[a] | Stockholm cordon pricing system[b] |
| Market research of catchment areas around road pricing projects to characterize users/assess equity. Additional equity evaluation results pre- and post-project implementation | |
| Information about tolling. For example, provide information to social agencies about tolls and options for avoiding tolls | Puget Sound,[c] San Francisco, SR 520 (Washington State) |
| Discuss and address "Lexus Lane" Concerns | Minneapolis[d] |
| Additional travel choice for drivers and educating users on the new transit options that will be available along the corridor | Los Angeles MTA[e] |
| Special groups' (ex. Truckers') concerns over negative effects of proposed pricing changes | New York[f] |

[a] Committee on the Equity of Transportation Finance Mechanisms, Equity of Evolving Transportation Finance Mechanisms, Transportation Research Board Special Report 303 (August 2011). http://onlinepubs.trb.org/onlinepubs/sr/sr303.pdf. Accessed Sept. 1, 2011.

[b] Taylor, B.D. How Fair Is Road Pricing? Evaluating Equity in Transportation Pricing and Finance. UCLA Institute of Transportation Studies, September 2010. http://www.bipartisanpolicy.org/sites/default/files/BPC%20Pricing%20EquityFIN.pdf. Accessed Jan. 20, 2012.

[c] Eight-Month Performance Summary of SR 167 High Occupancy Toll (HOT) Lanes Pilot Project (Washington State Department of Transportation, January 2008).

[d] Munnich, Lee W., Jr., and Kenneth R. Buckeye, I-394 MnPASS High-Occupancy Toll Lanes, Planning and Operational Issues and Outcomes, (Lessons Learned in Year 1). Transportation Research Record No. 1996: Journal of the Transportation Research Board, 2007.

[e] Los Angeles Region Express Lanes Project: AB 1467 Application (Los Angeles County Metropolitan Transportation Authority in partnership with the California Department of Transportation, March 2008).

[f] Report to the Traffic Congestion Mitigation Commission & Recommended Implementation Plan (New York City Traffic Congestion Mitigation Commission, January 2008). The new pricing scheme lifted peak hour prices dramatically but offered a substantial overnight discount on weekdays. While overnight truck traffic rose 2 percent, most truckers and trucking groups felt they had been unfairly targeted and that the special overnight discount was not helpful

**Table 7-2. What Equity-Related Messages to Communicate**

| Methods of Communication | |
|---|---|
| **Description** | **Example** |
| Emphasize communications throughout the entire project from planning to implementation. Develop and use communications plans describing how project information and impacts will be disseminated | • Numerous meetings and focus groups (Minneapolis)[a] |
| Foster community dialog and make communications two-sided. If changes can be made to a project based on citizen input then we want to disseminate information about a project and have live blogs and contact centers in order to inform the public and gather input | • Examples include an advisory task force, HOT lane workshop for Metropolitan Planning Organization (MPO) board members, and a press conference and public meetings early in the project planning. They suggest the need to foster community dialogue[b]<br>• Numerous policy advisory committees, community organizations, neighborhood groups, and business associations (San Francisco)[c] |

**Table 7-2. (Continued)**

| Methods of Communication | |
|---|---|
| **Description** | **Example** |
| | • Value Pricing Outreach Program including focus groups, discussions with community leaders, and board member education to promote the system. (Transportation Corridor Agencies, Southern California)[d] |
| Provide limited English proficiency (L.E.P.) plans and outreach in multiple languages as needed | • Washington State/SR 520 |
| Use a variety of public outreach and educational tools[e] | • Use surveys/focus groups/open houses to help identify designs most acceptable to public, refine strategies, and discuss concerns<br>• Advertise in newspapers, transit stations, online, and through neighborhood/business groups<br>• Social media strategies are emerging (e.g., Twitter, Facebook, YouTube)<br>• Internet, citizen champions, and a mobility coordinator role. (Dallas)f |
| Deploy a phased approach (small-scale [pilot] implementation first) to assess and then react to how users respond | • SF*park*, Stockholm |
| Contact majority with little to moderate outreach;<br>Contact a few with extensive outreach supporting long/incremental planning process | |
| Customer service centers | • SR 520 (Washington State) |
| A commercial video prepared to promote use of the facility | • SR 91 (Southern California),[g] LA Metro Express Lanes[h] |

[a] Munnich, Lee W., Jr., and Kenneth R. Buckeye, I-394 MnPASS High-Occupancy Toll Lanes, Planning and Operational Issues and Outcomes, (Lessons Learned in Year 1). Transportation Research Record No. 1996: Journal of the Transportation Research Board, 2007.

[b] Weinstein, A., and G. C. Sciara, Assessing the Equity Implications of HOT Lanes: A Report Prepared for the Santa Clara Valley Transportation Authority (San Jose

State University and University of California Berkeley, November 2004). http://www.vta.org/projects/hot_lanes/hot_equity.pdf. Accessed Sept. 1, 2011.

[c] San Francisco Mobility, Access and Pricing Study: Final Report (San Francisco County Transportation Authority, December 2010).

[d] Sullivan E., Continuation Study to Evaluate the Impacts of the SR-91 Value-Priced Lanes: Final Report (Cal Poly State University-San Luis Obispo, December 2000). See also Committee on the Equity of Transportation Finance Mechanisms, Equity of Evolving Transportation Finance Mechanisms, Transportation Research Board Special Report 303 (August 2011). http://onlinepubs.trb.org/onlinepubs/sr/sr303.pdf. Accessed Sept. 1, 2011.

[e] Private communication with MacGregor M., Texas Department of Transportation, CDA/Tollway Director, 2009.

[f] Sullivan E., Continuation Study to Evaluate the Impacts of the SR-91 Value-Priced Lanes: Final Report (Cal Poly State University-San Luis Obispo, December 2000).

[g] See: http://www.metro.net/projects/expresslanes/ . Accessed January 27, 2012. An updated video is to be made available in Spring 2012.

## 7.1. Congestion Pricing Communication Strategies – What and How, Illustrative Examples

For each of the road pricing scenarios described in Section 2.0, we provide examples of what to communicate and how to communicate it to stakeholders as well as interested and concerned parties.

| **Scenario 1: Agencies considering implementing roadway congestion pricing strategies for the first time** | |
|---|---|
| **What to communicate** | • Information about tolling<br>• Determining where and how revenues are used and how revenues will benefit roadway users<br>• Discuss and address potential equity concerns |
| **How to communicate** | • Emphasize communications throughout the entire project from planning to implementation<br>• Foster community dialog and make communications two-sided. If changes can be made to a project based on citizen input then we want to disseminate information about a project and have live blogs and contact centers in order to inform the public and gather input |
| **Description:** For regions new to road pricing, much of what they need is information. Why is a pricing strategy being recommended? How much will they be tolled and when and how? | |

**(Continued)**

| |
|---|
| If tolling will be facilitated with transponders, then how do they get a transponder? In addition to the logistics, the public should be told where and how revenues will be used and how the revenues will benefit roadway users. For regions where tolled lanes are referred to as "Lexus lanes," it is best to address that directly and explain that other road pricing projects are utilized by a mix of vehicles and drivers from all income classes. As with all road pricing projects, emphasizing communications to the public throughout the project including during initiation, planning, and implementation is vital. A variety of dissemination methods can be used including newspaper ads, press releases, websites, and community meetings. Ideally, community meetings and websites can be utilized to foster two-way communication. Project changes such as when the toll is charged or when the project opens may be initiated by community dialog. |

<table>
<tr><th colspan="2">Scenario 2: Agencies considering road pricing expansion along their network</th></tr>
<tr><td>What to communicate</td><td>• Market research of catchment areas around road pricing projects to characterize users/assess equity<br>• An additional travel choice for drivers and educating users on the new transit options that will be available along the corridor</td></tr>
<tr><td>How to communicate</td><td>• Schedule information sessions to educate the public and address concerns<br>• Inform the public about upcoming events and information related to the project through social media sites</td></tr>
<tr><td colspan="2">Description: Based upon city Y's experience with pricing, they will be able to communicate results of evaluations that show how users adjacent to priced roadways utilize the priced roadways. The agency will be able to communicate how groups are positively or negatively impacted by the priced roadway and they can communicate expected impacts of the new tolled roadways. Mature and new Express lane systems can also explain that the priced roadway provides an additional travel choice for drivers. In their communications, they can explain remediation measures like the addition of transit in the corridor. The system can also reach out to specific groups such as truckers and address their concerns explicitly. Similar to how these things can be communicated in county X, city Y can schedule information sessions to educate the public and address concerns. They can also update any project websites and provide information through social media sites including Twitter and Facebook.</td></tr>
</table>

# 8.0. Recommendations and Next Steps

In order to assist transportation agencies to better assess and mitigate equity impacts of road pricing projects on local communities, commuters, and system users, the FHWA developed this guidebook. This guidebook will help transportation agencies, decision-makers, and other interested parties, including the public, to better understand, address, and mitigate equity impacts of road pricing projects on local communities, commuters, and system users. The guidebook:

- Offers comprehensive procedures and guidance to State, regional, and local agencies, as well as decisionmakers and concerned citizens to follow when considering road pricing projects to ensure that equity issues are appropriately and adequately communicated, evaluated, and addressed to the best extent possible.
- Focuses primarily on time-of-day variable pricing applied to cordon and area-wide pricing, facility pricing (including high occupancy toll (HOT) lanes, express toll lanes, and traditional toll roads), and parking pricing. Was built upon:
  - A comprehensive literature review of existing road/congestion pricing equity research and applications;
  - A series of interviews with government staff, academics, private sector representatives, and other subject matter experts knowledgeable about road pricing equity; and
  - A workshop held in Washington D.C. in October 2011 to review and finalize the guidebook. The workshop was attended by road/congestion pricing and equity experts including government officials, researchers and academics, as well as private sector representatives.
- Includes two road pricing scenarios/case studies identified by FHWA. Two potential scenarios were introduced and used throughout the guidebook to illustrate potential applications of guidebook topics. These included:
  - Scenario 1: Agencies considering implementing roadway congestion pricing strategies for the first time.
  - Scenario 2: Agencies considering road pricing expansion along its network.

It is unlikely that any agency will be able to identify, evaluate, and remediate all potential equity issues resulting from new or ongoing road-pricing strategies and initiatives. There will likely be a degree of inequity in any project whether or not it involves road pricing. The point is to limit equity impacts or to work towards a new and more equitable system. Pricing projects may have positive impacts beyond users. The Miami 95 Express Lanes project reports improved travel times on the general purpose lanes adjacent to the HOT lanes suggesting that the project has improved travel for all in the corridor. By following this guidebook, agencies should be able to identify potential equity impacts, evaluate them, and identify remediation and communications methods that may address any identified equity impacts.

## 8.1. Recommendations

As a starting point, agencies may wish to keep the following guidelines in mind as they consider incorporating road pricing as an option into their planning processes:

- An analyst trained in equity can review the equity implications of all pricing concepts before they are discussed publicly, so that all agency officials are conversant with the major equity concepts in play.
- It may be helpful for agencies to first address the existing system and measure the equity of the existing system that the new policy or system will replace. No system is perfect in terms of equity. Incrementally, the new system should be more equitable than the existing system or policy it is replacing. Therefore, it is important to understand the pluses and minuses of the existing system to adequately address the pros and cons of the new system against the existing system in terms of horizontal and vertical equity.
- Mitigation measures will involve a package of transportation improvements almost inevitably including public transportation improvements. These packages should be developed at least at a high level before the discussion becomes public.
- Agencies may begin equity analysis by determining who is affected by the road pricing project. The agency may wish to provide targeted stakeholder outreach, specifically outreach to stakeholders who are likely to perceive greater equity harms. Agencies should avoid asking the question "What do you think of the new road pricing project?" in

isolation, as users will simply perceive it as an additional fee that they will have to pay. Instead, agencies may ask users to envision two futures—one with the road pricing project, and one without it, so that the users can understand the benefits and costs of each approach.

- Agencies can consider equity vs. efficiency tradeoffs present in the project. Broadly speaking the more completely equitable a project is, the less efficient (i.e., greater percentage of revenues needed to cover operating costs) it is.
- Agencies should focus on the net equity outcome. Often in analyzing a project, stakeholders, pubic officials, media, and members of the public tend to focus primarily on equity concerns that arise due to the project, and fail to recognize the equity problems that the project solves. The agency can demonstrate that net equity outcome is the key measure of effectiveness for the project.

## 8.2. Next Steps

***More Research and Analysis is Needed***

The literature review for this guidebook identified gaps related to equity and road pricing. The RAND study listed topics on equity impacts of congestion pricing. This literature review revealed a significant research gap in these topics. These topics include environmental justice impacts, long-term land use impacts of congestion pricing, equity implications of building new roads with congestion pricing revenue, and how adding congestion pricing to existing transportation finance mechanisms would change the equity implications.[32]

The August 2011 Special Report from the Transportation Research Board (TRB) suggests that comprehensive before-and-after studies are needed, as well as a better understanding of travel behavior and its consequences. It also recommends a knowledge base for decision support and a TRB Handbook for equity analyses of transportation finance policies.[33] It is hoped that the Guidebook developed in this project will come close to what TRB contemplates as an American Association of State Highway and Transportation Officials-funded National Cooperative Highway Research Program project. FHWA may be able to use resources like www.transportationresearch.gov_and the learning portal under development by the Intelligent Transportation Systems Professional Capacity Building program as the decision-support knowledge base that the TRB Committee envisioned.

# APPENDIX A. GLOSSARY

The terms in the glossary have been divided into the following subsections: key equity terms, types of equity, mitigation terms, key policy definitions, and other useful terms.

## Key Equity Terms

*Benefit principle*: The idea that it is equitable for one group to pay higher taxes if its members receive greater benefits.[34]

*Benefits received:* People who use a facility the most pay the most.[35]

*Classifications:* Ways that equity can be categorized in terms of what factors are taken into consideration

*Communications:* Working with the public in order to produce a favorable perspective and understanding of a road pricing project.

*Efficiency:* An allocation of resources is *efficient* if there is no other feasible allocation of resources that can make more people better off without making anyone worse off. In terms of transportation analyses, *efficiency* is measured in terms of a policy's ability to maximize overall total social welfare, regardless of whether some individuals are made worse off.

*Equality:* Distributing costs and benefits in a manner that benefits all people to the same extent. This can refer to *equality of opportunity,* whereby all people have the same chances, or *equality of outcome,* whereby all people end up with the same opportunities.[36]

*Equitable:* Meeting a normative standard of fairness.

*Equity:* A measure of "fairness" in terms of the distribution of costs and benefits among members of society. Such benefits and costs—whether monetary or nonmonetary—can be distributed in ways that people may see as reasonable or unreasonable.

*Equity categories:* The social groupings that are under observation.

*Equity impacts:* Consequences of transportation policy that may affect equity.

*Evaluation:* Examining road pricing projects in regard to various factors in order to assess their equity impacts.

*Impacts of concern:* The aspects of travelers' lives that are affected by the transportation or pricing project.

*Indicators*: Measurable variables selected to reflect progress toward planning objectives.

*Measures to assess equity impact*: To allow for comparison between projects or between the present situation and the future situation (after the project is built), the equity impacts must employ measures that account for the size of the project (e.g., per capita, per vehicle mile, per trip).

*Net equity outcome:* The positive and negative equity outcomes of a project—sometimes preferable to considering only negative outcomes.

*Polluter pays principle*: Tolls are considered fair if people pay an amount roughly equal to the costs they impose on others.[37]

*Remediation:* Strategies implemented to reduce inequity.

*Toll roads, bridges, and tunnels:* Individual routes that apply tolls independently. These facilities often collect tolls to repay bonds issued to finance their construction rather than to manage congestion. Tolls can be collected manually at tollbooths or electronically using *transponder* technology.

*Types of equity:* A set of criteria to constitute equal treatment.

*Units of analysis:* How equity is analyzed in regard to a particular group of individuals.

## Types of Equity

*Ability Equity*: concerning issues and inequalities effecting physically disabled persons.

*Access to tolled facilities equity*: A term[38] referring to whether barriers to owning a transponder, including requiring a credit cards (20 to 40 percent of U.S. households do not own credit cards) and large deposits, make using the facility too onerous.

*Compensatory equity:* Social problems and inequities addressed by providing transportation access or resources.

*Education equity:* concerning issues and inequalities facing less educated users in comparison to degree holders.

*Environmental/green equity:* Equal protection from environmental hazards for individuals, groups, or communities regardless of race, ethnicity, or economic status

*Gender equity:* A less recognized equity issue concerning the behavior and usage differences between male and female motorists (e.g., one study finds that women value travel-time reliability more than twice as highly as men).[39]

*Generational equity*: A subset of *vertical equity* concerning the burdens placed on future generations from policies made by and for the current generation. For example, borrowing for long-lived facilities is fair because it spreads the cost across generations of users, as opposed to current users paying for future generations.

*Geographic equity*: A subset of *vertical equity* concerning how where people work and live influences the effect transportation investment decisions has upon them (e.g., State versus state, urban versus rural).

*Horizontal equity:* How members of the same group (e.g., drivers or bus riders) fare relative to one another.

*Income equity*: Sometimes called *redistributive equity.* This equity type includes the effects on economically disadvantaged communities and low-income people. (e.g., do improvements negatively impact disadvantaged communities? Are improvements with negative consequences necessary for greater State or regional vitality?)

*Language equity:* concerns and inequalities faced by users not native to the standard language

*Life-stage equity:* concerning issues and inequalities faced by users of various life-stages in comparison to other users such as retirees, people with families, single users, etc.

*Market equity:* A price charged to each individual or group that is directly proportional to the costs imposed and benefits received by that individual or group.

*Modal equity*: Dedicating revenues to the modes where they were generated (e.g., a state requiring that gas tax revenue be spent on roads).

*Modal equity*: The effect on preferred travel behavior (e.g., Do activities conflict with public perceptions for the encouragement of multimodal transportation?).

*Occupancy equity:* concerning inequities and concerns faced by SOV users in comparison to HOV users (and vice versa).

*Opportunity equity:* Costs/benefits that are proportional to the size of the receiving group without regard to any other distinguishing characteristics between groups.

*Outcome equity:* See *vertical equity.*

*Participation equity:* Sometimes called *process equity*, the ability to participate in the decision-making related to a project by responding to a public solicitation, attending a public meeting, rallying neighbors to support or oppose a measure, and so on.

*Payment medium access equity:* Concern over a denial of access to priced road projects or reduced equity. A significant portion of the population does not have access to credit cards (20 to 40 percent of the population) or checking accounts (10 percent) that facilitate easier use of a road pricing facility. Others may find the deposits required to obtain a transponder onerous. Some toll roads require transponders.

*Process equity:* See *Participation equity*

*Race/ethnicity equity*: Considering whether different racial and ethnic groups, particularly minorities, are burdened disproportionately, taking into account fees paid, benefits received, and impacts experienced.

*Redistributive equity:* See *Income equity*

*Spatial equity*: A geographic application of the horizontal and vertical equity concepts.

*Vertical equity:* How members of different groups (e.g., low-income groups versus high-income groups, drivers versus non-drivers, or inner-city versus rural residents) fare relative to one another.

## Mitigation Terms

*All Electronic Tolling (AET):* Vehicles are automatically charged via transponder and license plate imaging

*Area-license systems*: Drivers may travel in and out of a zone an unlimited number of times for a fixed fee during certain hours. In addition, licensed residents of the zone may receive a discount or exemption.

*Cordon pricing:* Every time a vehicle crosses a boundary (i.e., cordon) into and out of a charged zone, a fee is charged. Generally, the amount of the charge varies between weekdays and weekends and peak and off-peak hours. Trips that begin and finish entirely within the zone are not charged.

*Credit-based congestion pricing*: Revenue-neutral pricing system in which an individual or group receives "credit" to charge toward a certain action such as traveling in congestion lanes during rush hour, or a certain amount of congestion fees to be used each month.

*Disability exemption:* Exemption offered to disabled individuals who may not have reasonable alternatives for transit (e.g., it is challenging or impossible for wheelchair users to use mass transit).

*Discounts*: Reductions in congestion charge offered to certain individuals or groups.

*Distance-based fees*: Vehicle use fees based on how many miles a vehicle is driven.

*Exemptions:* Excluding certain individuals or groups from being charged (e.g., emergency vehicles).

*Express lanes*: A variation on *HOT lanes* which carpools must pay a toll to use, though the toll may be lower than that charged to solo drivers.

*FAIR lanes:* Fast and Intertwined Regular Lanes, a variation on *HOT lanes* whereby drivers in the regular (un-tolled) lanes receive credits that, depending on the structure of the program, can be used to pay for using the fast (tolled) lanes, or for public transit fares or other transportation services.

*Geographic exemptions*: Exempting individuals from paying charges based on their residential/geographic situation (e.g., residents forced to drive through a cordoned zone regardless of their destination).

*HOT lanes:* High-occupancy/toll lanes, a version of high-occupancy vehicle (HOV) lanes. Qualified carpool vehicles can use HOT lanes free or at a discount, while other vehicles having must pay a toll. All vehicles continue to have the option of traveling in free general-purpose lanes.

*Income exemption:* Exempting individuals or groups from charges on the basis of their income level (e.g., household income less than $X is exempt).

*"Lexus Lanes":* A term used to describe road pricing projects as inequitable for lower income drivers. The term is effective and popular as a sound bite, but with has negative connotation for many.

*Revenue redistribution:* Redistributing revenues through public spending on specific transportation- related improvements.

*Road space rationing*: Using revenue-neutral credits to ration peak-period roadway capacity.

*Time-, distance-, and/or place-based pricing*: Adjusting road-user charges based on the distance traveled, location, time of day, and vehicle type. Some proposals also adjust the toll based on vehicle fuel efficiency or pollution certification level. These tolls are often collected to both finance maintenance efforts as well as manage congestion.

| -Based | Definition/Toll varies by… |
|---|---|
| Time- | time of day |
| Distance- | trip length |
| Place- | Facility type (bridge toll) |
| Fuel- | Electric vehicle may get a discount |
| Emissions- | Electric vehicle may get a discount |
| Vehicle type- | Trucks pay more |

*TOT lanes:* Truck only toll lanes, proposed to reduce traffic and congestion in the general purpose lanes by consolidating truck and freight operations into a separate facility

*Transit investment:* The use of transportation revenues to improve transit systems (thereby improving transportation choices for low-income travelers and those who are affected by new charges).

## Key Policy Definitions

*Civil Rights Restoration Act of 1987*: Identified the extent to which Title VI applied, to include all Federal- aid recipients, sub-recipients, and contractors, regardless of whether specific activities are federally funded or not.

*Environmental justice:* The fair treatment and meaningful involvement of all people regardless of race, color, national origin, or income with respect to the development, implementation, and enforcement of environmental laws, regulations, and policies (U.S. Environmental Protection Agency official definition).

*Executive Order 12898 of 1994*: Established the precedent that environmental justice consideration is extended to low-income populations and to avoid "disproportionately high and adverse" effects.

*Federal Aid Highway Act of 1970*: Ensured that transportation facilities would be approved "in the best overall public interest" with efforts to eliminate or minimize effects on community cohesion, employment effects, and displacement of people.

*National Environmental Policy Act of 1969*: An act requiring that for proposed major transportation facilities, an analysis of environmental impacts go beyond the infrastructure itself to include a broader geographic area.

*Title VI of the Civil Rights Act of 1964:* States that no person in the United States shall, on the ground of race, color, or national origin be excluded from participation in, be denied the benefits of, or be subjected to discrimination under any program or activity receiving Federal financial assistance.[40]

## Other Useful Terms

*Ability to Pay:* People who have more money pay more (i.e., a project is financed through a progressive tax that is paid disproportionately by higher income people).[41]

*Cost recovery:* The ratio between costs imposed on users and what they pay in user fees and special taxes.

*Costs imposed:* Users pay for the burden they impose on others (e.g., extra expense required to provide express bus service for suburb-to-city commuters is recovered through fares on this service).[42]

*"Do-Nothing Alternative"*: A solution where no action is taken.

*Equity audit tool*: A systematic approach to monitor and periodically make needed changes to implemented pricing programs to ensure that the tools to promote equitable outcomes are meeting their goals.[43]

*Focus groups:* Small groups of representative people who are questioned about their opinions as part of market research.

*Geographical Information System (GIS) analysis*—Often used to determine the location of groups affected by a project, and related to environmental justice concerns.

*Highway cost allocation*: Analysis of the costs imposed by various types of vehicles and the degree to which they are recovered by user fees.

*Limitation:* Maximum or minimum amount allowed.

*Mobility gap analysis*: An analysis of the difference in motorized travel (automobile, public transit, taxi, etc.) between households with and without automobiles ("zero-vehicle households").

*Process (or participation)*: Having a voice when the decision was made (e.g., Public outreach regarding proposed new high-occupancy toll lanes provides transparent information and seeks to involve all affected parties in public hearings and workshops.).[44]

*Progressive:* Placing a higher burden on those with higher incomes (e.g., the U.S. income tax).

*Regressive:* Placing a higher burden on those with lower incomes (e.g., a uniform tax of $500 is regressive, since $500 is a larger proportion of a lower income).

*Return to Source:* "We get back what we put in" (i.e., transit investment in each county is matched to that county's share of metropolitan tax revenues used for transit).[45]

*Revenue:* The income of a party from all sources, used to pay for the party's expenses.

*Revenue-neutral:* Having no effect on overall revenue.

*Subsidy:* A form of financial assistance paid to a business or economic sector.

*Surveys:* Examinations of opinions, behaviors, effects, and so on.

*Transponder:* A wireless communications, monitoring, or control device that picks up and automatically responds to an incoming signal.

*Unbanked:* Lacking access to a bank account either by choice or by circumstance.

*Uniform:* Treating all people equally from a strictly monetary perspective (e.g., a uniform tax would charge each person the same amount, and a uniform redistribution of revenues would provide each person with the same amount of money).

*Welfare:* The overall well-being of people, either as individuals or collectively.

In addition to the specific citations, the following sources were consulted in developing the glossary:

Texas Transportation Institute with assistance from Cambridge Systematics, *Background Paper #4: Equity, Fairness, and Uniformity in Tolling*, Washington State Comprehensive Tolling Study, Final Report, Volume 2, September 2006 (paper completed January 2006). http://www.wstc.wa.gov/Rates/Tolling/FR1_WS_TollStudy_Vol2_Paper04.pdf Accessed Sept. 1, 2011.

Ecola L. and Light T., Equity and Congestion Pricing A Review of the Evidence (RAND 2009).http://www.rand.org/pubs/technical_reports/TR680.html. Accessed January 27, 2012.

Equity of Evolving Transportation Finance Mechanisms, (Transportation Research Board Committee Special Report 303, 2011). http://onlinepubs.trb.org/onlinepubs/sr/sr303.pdf

King D. A., Remediating Inequity in Transportation Finance, (Transportation Research Board Special Report 303, 2009). http://onlinepubs.trb.org/onlinepubs/sr/sr303King.pdf Accessed Sept. 1, 2011.

Litman T., Evaluating Transportation Equity, World Transport Policy & Practice, Volume 8, No. 2, Summer 2002, pp. 50-65. Updated version (2011) available at http://www.islandnet.com/~litman/equity.pdf

Litman T., TDM Encyclopedia, VTPI, http://www.vtpi.org/tdm/tdm35.htm

# APPENDIX B. POTENTIAL REMEDIATION STRATEGIES

***Altering the Design of the Finance Policy***

- Price design limitations
- Increased access to transponders
- Park and ride facilities
- Revenues redistributed directly to collecting city
- Geographic system design
- Credit-based congestion pricing

***Giving Exemptions, Discounts, Subsidies, or Rebates to Parties Adversely Affected by the Policy***

- Discounts/exemptions
- Subsidies

***Offering or Improving Alternative Transportation Services***

- Revenue redistribution
- Increased access to alternative transit

***Policy Choices That Complicate Remediation Measures***

- All Electronic Tolling (AET)
- Long-term concession agreements; Public Private Partnerships
- Sales tax increase

## Altering the Design of the Finance Policy

| **Price Design Limitations** | |
|---|---|
| **Brief Description** | Identifying a maximum number of crossings that can be charged per time period. |
| **Deployment Sites** | New York City, Stockholm, Trondheim (Norway), Singapore |
| **Benefactors** | Frequent users |
| **Why this strategy is used** | May address spatial equity concerns and adverse impacts to one geographic area including drivers that due to the geography of their residency enter or exit the charged zone multiple times/day. |
| **Additional details** | Popular price design limitations include defining both the maximum allowed charge for each crossing and/or the maximum number of crossings that can be charged per period. Allowances may also be implemented allowing for unlimited use of priced facilities during certain periods (ex. holidays, weekends, off-peak hours). Inequities can arise in cordon pricing schemes due where some drivers, due to the geography of their residency, have no choice but to enter/exit the cordoned zone multiple times per day. Exemptions and/or placing a limit on the maximum number of crossings charged per day can address these inequities while still allowing the pricing in place to discourage others from driving in highly congested city centers. |
| **Links to more information** | Information about the Trondheim, Norway pricing system: http://www.progress-project.org/Progress/tron.html Information on congestion pricing trials in Stockholm, Sweden: http://www.stockholmsforsoket.se/templates/page.aspx?id=183 Paper about Singapore road pricing lessons learned: http://www.imprint-eu.org/public/Papers/IMPRINT3_chin.pdf TDM encyclopedia chapter on road pricing: http://www.vtpi.org/tdm/tdm35.htm |

**(Continued)**

| **Increased Access to Transponders/Stickers** | |
|---|---|
| **Brief Description** | Motorists can apply for and receive transponders at public assistance offices and other sites frequented by the general population including gas stations, and local retailers. |
| **Deployment Sites** | Puerto Rico (Auto Expreso System), Texas (TxTag), Washington (SR 520 bridge customer service centers), Minnesota (MnPASS), E-ZPASS (northeast US), Florida (SunPass), Seattle (Good To Go SR-520) |
| **Benefactors** | Low-income users |
| **Why this strategy is used** | People who only have access to cash and no stable bank account cannot pay with traditional transponder technology that is linked to a debit or credit card. Drivers need low cash deposit/no credit card necessary payment options. |
| **Additional details** | With some transponders, it is possible to reload with cash (i.e., Florida turnpike SunPass and AutoExpreso in Puerto Rico) at kiosks located at facilities and various retailers. This cash reload option allows for toll transponder benefits while still allowing use by the unbanked.<br>With an increasing number of toll plazas converting to all electronic tolling, increased access to transponder technology can greatly ease this transition. |
| **Links to more information** | Article about the wide availability of Florida SunPass transponders and where/how they can be paid for with cash: http://articles.sun-sentinel.com/2010-06-27/news/fl-sunpass-kiosks-20100625_1_sunpass-account-sunpass-mini-transponders<br>Information about Florida SunPass transponders: https://www.sunpass.com/index<br>Short article about SR520 Good-to-Go transponder availability: http://blog.seattlepi.com/transportation/2011/02/15/good-to-go-electronic-toll- passes-for-sr-520-now-available/<br>AutoExpreso (Puerto Rico) retail locations for obtaining AutoExpreso toolkit and replenishing toll amounts: https://www.autoexpreso.com |
| **Geographic System Design** | |
| **Brief Description** | Geographic system design applies mostly to cordon pricing. Under this strategy, cordon boundaries, exit points, etc. are purposefully located in ways that will maximize equity. |
| **Deployment Sites** | London and Stockholm (cordon boundaries), NYC cordon pricing |

| | |
|---|---|
| **Benefactors** | All drivers |
| **Why this strategy is used** | Maximize equity |
| **Additional details** | There may be a conflict between maximizing equity and maximizing revenue. Revenue concerns often trump equity concerns and cordon pricing schemes are likely to be designed with revenue as the top priority. |
| **Links to more information** | Income-Based Equity Impacts of Congestion Pricing: A Primer, FHWA: http://ops.fhwa.dot.gov/publications/fhwahop08040/fhwahop08040.pdf |
| **Credit-based Congestion Pricing** | |
| **Brief Description** | Drivers receive a monthly allowance of travel "credits" to be used on toll roads. Drivers only pay money "out of pocket" if they exceed their allowance. Drivers who spend less than their allowance can allow the credits to roll over for later use or exchange them for cash. Extra credits may be allotted to those with special, socially desirable, travel needs (ex. welfare-to-work participants, and single parent low-income household heads). |
| **Deployment Sites** | Pilot Sites:<br>• FAST Miles (tested statewide in Minnesota and in Austin, TX)<br>• HOT/C (HOT Credit) Lanes (tested in Alameda County, CA) |
| **Benefactors** | All drivers |
| **Why this strategy is used** | Strategy predicts increased transit use, peak travel to decrease, and total vehicle emissions to decrease. Potential to optimize network use and address equity, welfare, and revenue-distribution. |
| **Additional details** | Credit-based systems have not been implemented as of 2011 but feasibility testing has proved promising.<br>Implementation is easier with electronic toll collection. |
| **Links to more information** | Academic paper describing credit-based pricing: http://www.ce.utexas.edu/prof/kockelman/public_html/TR-A-CBCP.pdf HOT Credit Lanes Feasibility Study-Alameda County, CA, 2005: http://ops.fhwa.dot.gov/tolling_pricing/value_pricing/pubs_reports/projectreports/hot_credit_lanes.htm |

## Giving Exemptions, Discounts, Subsidies, or Rebates to Parties Adversely Affected by the Policy

| **Discounts/Exemptions** | |
|---|---|
| **Brief Description** | Discounts (reducing the amount of congestion charge paid) and exemptions (excluding certain persons or vehicles from payment) are often offered to certain types of vehicles and motorists with special transportation needs. |
| **Deployment Sites** | Widely implemented (most cities exempt transit and emergency vehicles), Milan and other cities also discount low-emission vehicles, London |
| **Benefactors** | Persons with special transportation needs and certain types of vehicles (ex. hybrid, emergency, military, law enforcement, etc.) |
| **Why this strategy is used** | Allow for unhindered travel of emergency personnel; encourage motorists to drive low- emission vehicles |
| **Additional details** | May have cost and enforcement consequences. The Los Angeles Metro Express Lanes have a Toll Credit Program that provides a $25 credit to low-income households (less than $35,000, twice the local poverty line) to be used towards either account transponder deposit or pre-paid tolls. Drivers in the Toll Credit Program will also have the $3 monthly account maintenance fee waived. |
| **Links to more information** | Potential Impact of Exempt Vehicles on HOV Lanes, FHWA: http://ops.fhwa.dot.gov/publications/exemptvehicleshov/chapter4.htm Information on Low Emission Zones for Italy & Germany: http://www.iema.net/news/envnews?aid=17943 Solo drivers of low-emission autos fume over fees to use carpool lanes, LA Times: http://articles.latimes.com/2011/sep/14/business/la-fi-autos-carpool-20110914 Academic paper on lessons learned from road pricing in London: http://onlinelibrary.wiley.com/doi/10.1111/j.1468-0327.2006.00159.x/abstract;jsessionid=DCD5887FCE108B1D8E78B0726F6A797D.d03t03 Discounts and exemptions for London charging zone: http://www.tfl.gov.uk/roadusers/congestioncharging/6713.aspx Los Angeles Metro Toll Credit Program http://www.metro.net/projects/expresslanes/ |

| Subsidies | |
|---|---|
| **Brief Description** | A portion of revenue from the project is used to subsidize the toll cost/costs of low- income commuters or transit. |
| **Deployment Sites** | Central Texas toll roads (Texas 130, Loop 1, Texas 45N), Germany and France (taxpayers can deduct commuting expenses from their income tax liability) |
| **Benefactors** | Low-income commuters |
| **Why this strategy is used** | Encourage use of facilities by low-income population |
| **Additional details** | Not widely implemented, it is more likely that low-income commuters will be offered a discount up front rather than receive a subsidy. Toll revenue is also more likely to be diverted to the low-income community through improvements to low-income transit options. Subsidy proposals are often not well received by the general population. |
| **Links to more information** | Tolls would subsidize rail line along Route 422, Chester County Daily Local News: http://www.dailylocal.com/article/20110919/NEWS/309199941/tolls-would-subsidize- rail-line-along-route-422<br>Using Drivers' Tolls to Subsidize Light Rail across the Columbia River is Wrong, The Columbian-Op/Ed section: http://www.washingtonpolicy.org/publications/opinion/using-drivers-tolls-subsidize- light-rail-across-columbia-river-wrong |

## Offering or Improving Alternative Transportation Services

| Revenue Redistribution | |
|---|---|
| **Brief Description** | Revenue from facility is redistributed through public spending on specific transportation-related improvements. |
| **Deployment Sites** | Widely implemented (common practice among recent pricing projects) I-15 in San Diego (funds support express bus service), Norwegian toll rings (funds support roadway/transit improvement) |
| **Benefactors** | All commuters |
| **Why this strategy is used** | Revenue is used to make improvements to facilities, roads, etc. to benefit and provide additional travel modes to all corridor users. |
| **Additional details** | |

**(Continued)**

| | |
|---|---|
| **Links to more information** | |
| **Increased Access to Alternative Transit** | |
| **Brief Description** | Transit, vanpools, paratransit, or other options as alternatives in locations not served by mass transit. Expand existing facilities to serve more people. |
| **Deployment Sites** | Widely implemented, Washington State light rail expansion, Campus carsharing/ridesharing programs (message-boards & social media to connect people to transit)<br>Miami (Dade and Broward Counties), I-95 Express Lanes introduced significant new Bus Rapid Transit service in the corridor in advance of opening of Phase 1. This new service, coupled with dramatic improvement in travel speeds in the managed lanes, resulted in a 145% increase in ridership in the first two years of the project. |
| **Benefactors** | Non-drivers, Choice transit riders (those who own cars), All drivers (congestion reduction) |
| **Why this strategy is used** | Reduce congestion in urban areas and potentially share/split toll rates. |
| **Additional details** | |
| **Links to more information** | Information on Puget Sound (Washington) Transit Capital projects:<br>http://projects.soundtransit.org/<br>Virginia Tech alternative transportation information:<br>http://www.facilities.vt.edu/tcs/alternative/ |
| **Sales Tax Increase** | |
| **Brief Description** | Under this strategy, sales tax is increased in order to fund transit and infrastructure rather than relying solely on revenue generated by pricing projects. |
| **Deployment Sites** | Massachusetts (2009), Durham County, NC (2011) |
| **Benefactors** | Users of public transportation (transit projects receive funding from sales tax more often than roadway projects) |
| **Why this strategy is used** | This has been argued as a more equitable as all residents are charged equally based on their purchases. Sales tax is also a fairly reliable source of revenue during uncertain economic periods and can make up for budget shortfalls. |

| **Additional details** | |
|---|---|
| **Links to more information** | Brief on regions that fund transit with sales tax: http://www.tlcminnesota.org/pdf/Sources%20of%20funding%20for%20public%20transit%202009%20Final%20April%2021.pdf<br>Durham voters approve sales tax increase for transit, Triangle Business Journal: http://www.bizjournals.com/triangle/news/2011/11/09/durham-voters-approve-sales- tax.html<br>Mass. Senate OKs transportation bill that includes sales tax increase, no toll or gas tax increase, Masslive.com article,2009: http://www.masslive.com/news/index.ssf/2009/06/mass_senate_oks_transportation.h tml<br>Possible Sales Tax Increase to Help Fund Public Transportation: http://nwahomepage.com/fulltext-news/?nxd_id=287497 |

## APPENDIX C. BIBLIOGRAPHY

407 ETR. "407 Express Toll Route" [All electronic tolling; Ontario]. http://www.407etr.com/index.html

Algers, S; Brundell Freij, K; et al. "*The Stockholm Congestion Charging Trial—What Happened*?" http://www.stockholmsforsoket.se/upload/Rapporter/Expert_group_summary_060621.pdf

Altshuler, A. "Equity, Pricing, and Surface Transportation Politics." *Paper commissioned for Transportation Research Board Special Report 303*. 2010. http://onlinepubs.trb.org/onlinepubs/sr/sr303Altshuler.pdf

Anderson, D; Mohring, H. "Congestion Costs and Congestion Pricing." In *The Full Costs and Benefits of Transportation: Contributions to Theory, Method and Measurement* (J. D. Greene, D. W. Jones, and M. A. Delucchi, eds.) New York, Springer 1997.

Bagley, C. "Durham Voters Approve Sales Tax Increase for Transit." *Triangle Business Journal*. The Business Journals Digital Network. November 9, 2011. http://www.bizjournals.com/triangle/news/2011/11/09/durham-voters-approve-sales-tax.html

Baker, R; et al. "Moving Beyond Lexus Lanes: Equity Considerations for Managed Lanes." Transportation Research Board 87th Annual Meeting, 2008. http://pubsindex.trb.org/view.aspx?id=848563

Bayles, F. "Toll Lanes: A Freer Ride, for a Price." *USA Today*, April 9, 2004. http://www.usatoday.com/news/nation/2004-04-07-tolls-usat_x.htm

Berg, J; Bhatt, K; Higgins T. *Value Pricing Pilot Program: Lessons Learned Final Report* (KTA & CSI, 2008). http://ops.fhwa.dot.gov/publications/fhwahop08023/vppp_lessonslearned.pdf

Boehm, E. "Tolls Would Subsidize Rail Line along Route 422," Dailylocal.com. *Daily Local News : Serving Chester County*. September 19, 2011. http://www.dailylocal.com/article/20110919/NEWS/309199941/tolls-would-subsidize-rail-line- along-route-422

Bonsall, P; Kelly, C. "Road User Charging and Social Exclusion: The Impact of Congestion Charges on At-Risk Groups." *Transport Policy*, Vol. 12, No. 5, 2005, 406–18.

Bork, R; Wrede, M. "Political economy of commuting subsidies." *Journal of Urban Economics* No. 57, 2005, 478–99. http://pdfcast.org/pdf/ political-economy-of-commuting-subsidies

Burris, M; Hannay, R. "Equity Analysis of the Houston Quickride Project." *Transportation Research Record 1859*. March 2003. https://ceprofs.civil.tamu.edu/mburris/Papers/TRR%201859%20-%20EQUITY%20ANALYSIS%20OF%20THE%20HOUSTON,%20TEXAS,%20QUICKRIDE%20PROJECT.pdf

Burt, M; Sowell, G; Crawford, J; Carlson, T. *Synthesis of Congestion Pricing-Related Environmental Impact Analyses – Final Report.* 2010. http://www.ops.fhwa.dot.gov/publications/fhwahop11008/index.htm

Carlson, D; Howard, Z. *Impacts of VMT Reduction Strategies on Selected Areas and Groups.* Washington State Department of Transportation, 2010. www.wsdot.wa.gov/research/reports/fullreports/751.1.pdf

Committee on the Equity of Transportation Finance Mechanisms. *Equity of Evolving Transportation Finance Mechanisms.* Transportation Research Board Special Report 303 (August 2011). http://onlinepubs.trb.org/onlinepubs/sr/sr303.pdf

DeCorla-Souza, P. "Fair Highway Networks: A New Approach to Eliminate Congestion on *Metropolitan Freeways,"* Public Works Management and Policy, Vol. *9*, No. 3, 2005, 196–205.

DeCorla-Souza, P. "Improving Metropolitan Transportation Efficiency with Fast Miles." *Journal of PublicTransportation,* Vol. 9, No. 1, 2006, 45–70.

E-470 Public Highway Authority. "E-470." https://www.expresstoll.com/Pages/Home.aspx

Ecola, L; Light, T. *Equity and Congestion Pricing: A Review of the Evidence* RAND. 2009. http://www.rand.org/pubs/technical_reports/TR680.html

Eichler, MD; Miller, GK; Park. J. *Evaluating Alternative Scenarios for a Network of Variably Priced Highway Lanes in the Metropolitan Washington Region—Final Report* February 2008. http://www.mwcog.org/uploads/committee-documents/aF5fWVlW20080314161420.pdf

Land Transport Authority of Singapore. "*Electronic Road Pricing.*" http://www.lta.gov.sg/content/ltaweb/en/roads-and-motoring/managing-traffic-and- congestion/electronic-road-pricing-erp.html

Ennis, M. "Using Drivers' Tolls to Subsidize Light Rail across the Columbia River Is Wrong" Washington Policy Center. March 13, 2011. http://www.washingtonpolicy.org/publications/opinion/using-drivers-tolls-subsidize-light-rail-across-columbia-river-wrong.

FHWA. *Income-Based Equity Impacts of Congestion Pricing: A Primer.* FHWA-HOP-08-040. 2009. http://www.ops.fhwa.dot.gov/publications/fhwahop08040/fhwahop08040.pdf

FHWA. *Potential Impact of Exempt Vehicles on HOV Lanes.* "Chapter Four—HOV Exemptions for Law Enforcement and Public Transportation Vehicles." FHWA-HOP-05-058. August 2005. http://ops.fhwa.dot.gov/publications/exemptvehicleshov/chapter4.htm

FHWA. "*The Role of Fast and Intertwined Regular (FAIR) Lanes in the New York Metropolitan Region.*" Conference proceedings. 2002. http://ops.fhwa.dot.gov/tolling_pricing/value_pricing/fairlanes.htm

FHWA Office of Innovative Program Delivery. "*Project Profiles: Indiana Toll Road.*" http://www.fhwa.dot.gov/ipd/project_profiles/in_indianatoll.htm

FHWA Office of Innovative Program Delivery. "*Project Profiles: New-Build Facilities.*" http://www.fhwa.dot.gov/ipd/p3/project_profiles/index.htm

FHWA and TxDOT, *"Joint Guidance for Project and Network Level Environmental Justice, Regional Network Land Use, and Air Quality Analyses for Toll Roads.*" April 23, 2009. [Obtained by email between Anita Wilson and Patrick DeCorla-Souza, FHWA]

Florida's Turnpike Enterprise. "*All-Electronic Open Road Tolling.*" http://www.floridasturnpike.com/all- electronictolling/

Franklin, J. "*The Equity Effects of Roadway Tolls: An Application of Hicksian Welfare Measures with Income Effects.*" Conference Paper Workshop 2.4. Proc., International Conference on Travel Behaviour Research, Kyoto, Japan, Aug. 16–20, 2006. http://www.urbansim.org/pub/Research/ResearchPapers/franklin-2006-iatbr.pdf

Fridström, L; Minken, H; Moilanen, P; Shepherd, S; Vold, A. *Economic and Equity Effects of Marginal Cost Pricing in Transport: Case Studies from*

*Three European Cities*. Technical Report. (Helsinki, Finland: Government Institute for Economic Research) 2000.

Giuliano, G; et al. *Pricing & Social Equity: Road Pricing & Barriers to Social Inclusion*. USC SPPD Keston Institute. April 16. 2010. http://www.youtube.com/watch?v=zmqF_DmuICQ

Glaister, S. "National Road Pricing: Policy Design and Public Acceptance." Paper presented at International Trade Center–Co-Ordination of Urban Road-User Charging Organizational Issues. 2007.

Glaister, S; Graham, D. "An Evaluation of National Road User Charging in England." *Transportation Research Part A*, Vol. 39, 2005, 632–50.

Gomez-Ibanez, JA. "The Political Economy of Highway Tolls and Congestion Pricing." *Transportation Quarterly* XLVI, No. 2, July 1992.

Gonzales, EJ. "Efficiency and Equity of Pricing Strategies for Cars and Transit." Presentation at TRB Annual Meeting. January 2012.

Goodin, G; Poole, R; Fuhs, C; Tsien, J; Lee, J. *I-405/SR 167 Corridor Tolling Study Expert Review Panel Final Report*. December 2010. http://www.wsdot.wa.gov/NR/rdonlyres/EBD4BC88-9606-4388-92BA-B862AA566CEC/72822/405ExpertReviewFinalReport_a.pdf

Goodwin, P. "The Rule of Three: A Possible Solution to the Political Problem of Competing Objectives for Road Pricing." *Traffic Engineering and Control*, Vol. 30, No. 10, 1989, 495–97.

Gutierrez, S. "Good to Go! Electronic Toll Passes for SR 520 Now Available." *Blogs - Seattlepi.com*. February 15, 2011. http://blog.seattlepi.com/transportation/2011/02/15/good-to-go-electronic- toll-passes-for-sr-520-now-available/

Hamer, P; Currie, G; Young, W. "Equity Implications of Parking Taxes," Presentation at TRB Annual Meeting 2012. January 2012.

Hirsch, J. "Solo Drivers of Low-emission Autos Fume over Fees to Use Carpool Lanes - Los Angeles Times." The Los Angeles Times, September 14, 2011. http://articles.latimes.com/2011/sep/14/business/la-fi-autos-carpool-20110914

ICF International. *Environmental Justice in Transportation: Emerging Trends and Best Practices*. FHWA. 2011. http://www.fhwa.dot.gov/environment/ejustice/lib/guidebook/index.cfm

Institute for Transport Studies, University of Leeds. "Coordination of Urban Road User Charging Organisational Issues." *State of the Art Review*." May 2009.

Institute for Transport Studies, University of Leeds. "Equity." *State of the Art Review*. April 1, 2006.

Leromonachou, P; Potter, S; Warren, JP. “Norway’s Urban Toll Rings: Evolving Towards Congestion Charging?” *Transport Policy*, Vol. *13*, No. 5, September 2006, 367–78.

Institute of Environmental Management and Assessment. *Low Emission Zones for Italy and Germany*. January 2, 2008. http://www.iema.net/news/envnews?aid=17943

Johnson, G. "Mass. Senate OKs Transportation Bill That Includes Sales Tax Increase, No Toll or Gas Tax Increase.” *Masslive.com*. June 18, 2009. http://www.masslive.com/news/index.ssf/2009/06/mass_senate_oks_transportation.html

Johnston, RA; Rodier, CJ.”Synergisms Among Land Use, Transit, and Travel Pricing Policies.” *Transportation Research Record: Journal of the Transportation Research Board*, No. 1670, 1999, 3–7.

King County Metro Transit. “King County Park & Ride Lot Information." http://metro.kingcounty.gov/tops/parknride/parknride.html

King, DA. “Remediating Inequity in Transportation Finance.” Paper commissioned for Transportation Research Board Special Report 303. 2009. http://onlinepubs.trb.org/onlinepubs/sr/sr303King.pdf

King, DA; Manville, M; Shoup, D. “For Whom the Road Tolls.” *Access* (University of California Transportation Center) No. 31, 2007. http://shoup.bol.ucla.edu/ForWhomTheRoadTolls.pdf

King, DA; Manville, M; Shoup, D. “The Political Calculus of Congestion Pricing.” *Transport Policy*, Vol. *14*, No. 2, March 2007, 111–23. http://shoup.bol.ucla.edu/PoliticalCalculus.pdf

Klein, DB; Fielding, GJ. “Private Toll Roads: Learning from the 19th Century.” *Transportation Quarterly*. Vol. *46*, No. 3, July 1992, 321–41.

Kockelman, KM; Kalmanje, S. “Credit-Based Congestion Pricing: A Policy Proposal and the Public’s Response.” *Transportation Research Part A: Policy and Practice*. Vol. *39*, No. 7–9, August– November 2005.

K.T. Analytics and Cambridge Systematics. *Value Pricing Pilot Program: Lessons Learned*. FHWA, August 2008. http://www.ops.fhwa.dot.gov/publications/fhwahop08023/vppp_lessonslearned.pdf

Lam, TC; Small, KA. “The Value of Time and Reliability: Measurement from a Value Pricing Experiment.” *Transportation Research Part E*, Vol. 37, No. 2–3, 2001, 231–51.

Larsen, L; Burris, M; et al. “Equity Evaluation of Vehicle Miles Traveled Fees in Texas,” Presentation at TRB Annual Meeting. January 2012.

The Leadership Conference Education Fund. *Where We Need to Go: A Civil Rights Roadmap for Transportation Equity*. March 2011.

http://www.protectcivilrights.org/pdf/docs/transportation/52846576-Where-We-Need-to-Go-A-Civil-Rights-Roadmap-for-Transportation-Equity.pdf

Levinson, D. “Equity Effects of Road Pricing: A Review.” *Transport Reviews*, Vo. 30, No. 1, 2010, 33— 57. http://dx.doi.org/10.1080/01441640903189304

Litman, T. *Changing Vehicle Travel Price Sensitivities: The Rebounding Rebound Effect.* Victoria Transport Policy Institute, 2010. http://www.vtpi.org/VMT_Elasticities.pdf

Litman, T. “Evaluating Transportation Equity.” *World Transport Policy & Practice.* Vol. *8*, No. 2, Summer 2002, 50–65. Updated version (May 2011). http://www.islandnet.com/~litman/equity.pdf

Litman, T. "Park & Ride." *Online TDM Encyclopedia.* Victoria Transport Policy Institute, January 26, 2010. http://www.vtpi.org/tdm/tdm27.htm

Litman, T. "Road Pricing-Congestion Pricing, Value Pricing, Toll Roads, and HOT Lanes." *Online TDM Encyclopedia.* Victoria Transport Policy Institute. June 9, 2011. http://www.vtpi.org/tdm/tdm35.htm

Litman, T. *Smart Transportation Investments: Reevaluating the Role of Highway Expansion for Improving Urban Transportation.* Victoria Transport Policy Institute. October 1, 2006. http://www.vtpi.org/cong_relief.pdf

Litman, T. *Transportation Affordability: Evaluation and Improvement Strategies.* Victoria Transport Policy Institute. 2011. www.vtpi.org/affordability.pdf

Litman, T. *Using Road Pricing Revenue: Economic Efficiency and Equity Considerations.* Victoria Transport Policy Institute. February 2010. http://www.vtpi.org/revenue.pdf

Litman, T; Brenman, M. *A New Social Equity Agenda for Sustainable Transportation.* Victoria Transport Policy Institute. March 2011. http://www.vtpi.org/equityagenda.pdf

Lloyd, G. "Voters to Decide on Sales Tax." *The Chronicle.* Duke University. (n.d.) http://dukechronicle.com/article/voters-decide-sales-tax

Los Angeles County Metropolitan Transportation Authority in partnership with the California Department of Transportation. *Los Angeles Region Express Lanes Project: AB 1467 Application.* March 2008.

Los Angeles Metro. "Park & Ride Lots." http://www.metro.net/around/paid_parking/.

Maruyama, T; Sumalee, A. "Efficiency and Equity Comparison of Cordon- and Area-Based Road Pricing Schemes Using A Trip-Chain Equilibrium Model." *Transportation Research Part A.* Vol. 41, No. 7, 2007, 655–71.

Maryland DOT State Highway Administration. *The Intercounty Connector.* http://www.iccproject.com/

*MDXWay*. Miami-Dade Expressway Authority. http://www.mdx-way.com/

Metropolitan Washington Council of Governments. "Park and Ride Lot Locations." *Commuter Connections.* http://www.mwcog.org/commuter2/commuter/ridesharing/prlocations.html

Mitchell, G. "Forecasting Environmental Equity: Air Quality Responses to Road User Charging in Leeds, UK." *Journal of Environmental Management*, Vol. 77, No. 3, 2005, 212–26.

Mohring, H. "Congestion." In *Essays in Transportation Economics and Policy: A Handbook in Honor of John R. Meyer* (J. Gomez-Ibanez, W. Tye and C. Winston, eds.) Washington, DC: Brookings Institution Press, 1999, 181–222.

Munnich, LW Jr.; Buckeye, KR. "I-394 MnPASS High-Occupancy Toll Lanes, Planning and Operational Issues and Outcomes (Lessons Learned in Year 1)." *Transportation Research Record No. 1996: Journal of the Transportation Research Board*, 2007.

Nakamura, K; Kockelman, K. "Congestion Pricing and Roadspace Rationing: An Application to the San Francisco Bay Bridge Corridor." *Transportation Research Part A*, Vol. 36, No. 5, 2002, 403–17.

New York City Traffic Congestion Mitigation Commission. *Report to the Traffic Congestion Mitigation Commission & Recommended Implementation Plan.* January 2008.

North Texas Tollway Authority. "Cashless Tolling (all-ETC)." http://www.ntta.org/AboutUs/Projects/AllETC/

North Texas Tollway Authority. "Open for Business: Sam Rayburn Tollway & Dallas North Tollway Interchange 'Making Travel Better.'" http://www.ntta.org/

Office of Policy and Governmental Affairs. "Project Descriptions." *FHWA.* April 5, 2011.

Parkany, E. "Environmental Justice Issues Related to Transponder Ownership and Road Pricing." *Transportation Research Record, a Journal of the Transportation Research Board 1932*, 2005, 97–108.

Parsons Brinckerhoff Quade & Douglas, Inc., et al. "HOT Credit Lanes Feasibility Study." Alameda County Congestion Management Agency.

August 2005. http://ops.fhwa.dot.gov/tolling_pricing/value_pricing/pubs_reports/projectreports/hot_credit_l anes.htm

The Pennsylvania Turnpike. "All Electronic Tolling (AET)-How Does It Work?" *AET Feasibility Study.* http://www.paturnpike.com/aet_public/aet.asp

The Pennsylvania Turnpike. "Welcome to E-ZPass on the Pennsylvania Turnpike." http://www.paturnpike.com/ezpass/ezpassINTRO.htm

Plotnick, R; Romich, J; Thacker, J. *The Impacts of Tolling on Low-Income Persons in the Puget Sound Region.* University of Washington, April 2009. http://www.wsdot.wa.gov/research/reports/fullreports/721.1.pdf

Private communication with MacGregor, M. Texas Department of Transportation, CDA/Tollway Director, 2009.

Progress Project. "Trondheim (Norway)." http://www.progress-project.org/Progress/tron.html

Pucher, J; Renne, JL. "Socioeconomics of Urban Travel: Evidence from the 2001 NHTS." *Transportation Quarterly*, Vol. *57*, No. 3, Summer 2003, 49–77. http://nhts.ornl.gov/2001/articles/socioeconomicsOfUrbanTravel.pdf

Riverside County Transportation Commission. "SR-91 Project." *SR-91 Corridor Improvement Project.* http://rctc.org/projects/state-route-91/sr-91-corridor-improvement-project

Robinson, G; Kuzmyak, R; Sanchez, T. *Filling the Gap: Environmental Justice in Transportation Toolkit.* Federal Transit Administration, May 2007. http://www.scribd.com/doc/10961106/tecrptaski3bts

Rodier, C; Abraham, JE; Dix, BN; Hunt, JD. *Equity Analysis of Land Use and Transport Plans Using an Integrated Spatial Model*, Report 09-08. Mineta Transportation Institute, 2010. www.transweb.sjsu.edu/MTIportal/research/publications/documents/Equity%20Analysis%20of%20Land%20Use%20(with%20Covers).pdf

Rosenbloom, S. "The Equity Implications of Financing the Nation's Surface Transportation System." *TR News*, No. 261, March–April 2009, 3–9.

Safirova, E; Gillingham, K; Parry, I; et al. *Welfare and Distributional Effects of Road Pricing Schemes for Metropolitan Washington, DC.* October 2003. http://www.rff.org/RFF/Documents/RFF-DP-03- 57.pdf

San Francisco County Transportation Authority. *San Francisco Mobility, Access and Pricing Study: Final Report.* December 2010.

San Francisco Department of Public Health, Program on Health Equity and Sustainability. *Assessing the Health Impacts of Road Pricing Policy Proposals*. 2010.

Santos, G; Fraser, G. “Road pricing: lessons from London.” *Economic Policy.* Vol. *21*, Is. 46, 2006, 263–310. http://onlinelibrary.wiley.com/doi/10.1111/j.1468-0327.2006.00159.x/abstract;jsessionid=3BA0639AA164C0DF2E3A66008BFDD0B8.d02t01.

Schweitzer, L. “The Empirical Research on the Social Equity of Gas Taxes, Emissions Fees, and Congestion Charges,” Paper commissioned for Transportation Research Board Committee Special Report 303. 2009. http://onlinepubs.trb.org/onlinepubs/sr/sr303Schweitzer.pdf

Schweitzer, L; Taylor, B. “Just Pricing: The Distributional Effects of Congestion Pricing and Sales Taxes.” *Transportation*, Vol. 35, No. 6, 2008, 797–812.

Seattle Department of Transportation. *Seattle Variable Tolling Study.* May 2009. http://www.seattle.gov/transportation/docs/FINAL%20Tolling%20Study%20report%20revised% 206.25.10.pdf

Skyway Concession Company. "Chicago Skyway." 2005. http://www.chicagoskyway.org/

Small, K. Using the Revenues from Congestion Pricing. *Transportation.* Vol. 19, No. 4, 1992, 359-381.

Sound Transit. "Sound Transit Capital Projects." http://projects.soundtransit.org/

Space Coast Area Transit. http://www.ridescat.com/

Steininger, K; Friedl, B; Gebetsroither, B. “Sustainability Impacts of Car Road Pricing: A Computable General Equilibrium Analysis for Austria.” *Ecological Economics*. Vol. *63*, No. 1, 2007, 59–69.

Stevens, M. "Possible Sales Tax Increase to Help Fund Public Transportation." *Nwa.com.* November 22, 2011. http://nwahomepage.com/fulltext-news/?nxd_id=287497.

"The Stockholm Trials 22 August 2005 - 31 July 2006." *Stockholmsförsöket.* http://www.stockholmsforsoket.se/templates/page.aspx?id=183.

Sullivan, E. *Continuation Study to Evaluate the Impacts of the SR-91 Value-Priced Lanes: Final Report.* Cal Poly State University-San Luis Obispo, December 2000.

Swan, PF; Belzer, MH. “Empirical Evidence of Toll Road Traffic Diversion and Implications for Highway Infrastructure Privatization.” *Public Works Management and Policy*, Vol. *14*, No. 4, 2010, 351–73.

Tampa-Hillsborough Expressway Authority. *Selmon Expressway.* http://www.tampa-xway.com/.

Taylor, BD. *How Fair is Road Pricing? Evaluating Equity in Transportation Pricing and Finance.* UCLA Institute of Transportation Studies.

September 2010. http://www.bipartisanpolicy.org/sites/default/files/BPC%20Pricing%20EquityFIN.pdf

Teubel, U. "The Welfare Effects and Distributional Impacts of Road User Charges on Commuters—An Empirical Analysis of Dresden." *International Journal of Transport Economics.* Vol. 27, 2000, 231–55.

Texas Transportation Institute with assistance from Cambridge Systematics. "Background Paper #4: Equity, Fairness, and Uniformity in Tolling." *Washington State Comprehensive Tolling Study, Final Report, Volume* 2. September 2006. http://www.wstc.wa.gov/Rates/Tolling/FR1_WS_TollStudy_Vol2_Paper04.pdf

Toups, DT. San Diego Association of Governments. FasTrak Study—Follow-Up Questions. E-mail to Liisa Ecola, December 18, 2008.

Transit for Livable Communities. "Most Regions Fund Transit with Sales Tax." *A Transit for Livable Communities Policy Brief.* April 2009. http://www.tlcminnesota.org/pdf/Sources%20of%20funding%20for%20public%20transit%2020 09%20Final%20April%2021.pdf

Transport for London. "Discounts and Exemptions." http://www.cclondon.com/exemptions.shtml

Turnbell, M. "Florida Drivers Can Use Cash Now to Reload SunPass Transponders." *The Sun Sentinel.* June 27, 2010. http://articles.sun-sentinel.com/2010-06-27/news/fl-sunpass-kiosks- 20100625_1_sunpass-account-sunpass-mini-transponders

Ungemah, DH. "This Land Is Your Land, This Land Is My Land: Addressing Equity and Fairness in Tolling and Pricing." *Transportation Research Record.* Vol. *2013*, 2007, 13–20.

Victoria Transport Policy Institute. *Evaluating Pricing Strategies: Factors To Consider when Evaluating TDM Strategies that Change Transportation Prices.* Victoria, B.C.: Victoria Transport Policy Institute, May 2010. http://www.vtpi.org/tdm/tdm70.htm

Virginia Tech Facilities Services. "Alternative Transportation." 2010. http://www.facilities.vt.edu/tcs/alternative/

Washington State Department of Transportation. *Eight-Month Performance Summary of SR 167 High Occupancy Toll (HOT) Lanes Pilot Project.* January 2008.

Wear, B. "Central Texas Toll Roads Need More State Subsidies than Expected." *The Austin-American Statesman.* July 18, 2011. http://www.statesman.com/news/local/central-texas-toll-roads-need-more-state-subsidies-1618544.html

Weinstein, A; Sciara, GC. *Assessing the Equity Implications of HOT Lanes: A Report Prepared for the Santa Clara Valley Transportation Authority.* San Jose State University and University of California Berkeley. November 2004. http://www.vta.org/projects/hot_lanes/hot_equity.pdf

Weinstein, A; Sciara, GC. "Unraveling Equity in HOT Lane Planning: A View from Practice." *Journal of Planning Education and Research.* No. *26*, 2006, 174–184.

West, S. "The Incidence of Public Finance Schemes." Paper commissioned for Transportation Research Board Committee Special Report 303. 2009. http://onlinepubs.trb.org/onlinepubs/sr/sr303West.pdf

Whitty, J; Imholt, B. *Oregon's Mileage Fee Concept and Road User Fee Pilot Program: Report to the 73rd Oregon Legislative Assembly on Proposed Alternatives to the Current System of Taxing Highway Use Through Motor Vehicle Fuel Taxes.* Salem: Oregon Legislative Assembly, 2005. http://www.oregon.gov/ODOT/HWY/OIPP/docs/2005LegislativeReport.pdf.

Zhang, L; Levinson, D; Zhu, S. "Agent-Based Model of Price Competition, Capacity Choice, and Product Differentiation on Congested Networks." *Journal of Transport Economics and Policy.* Vol. *42*, No. 3, 2008, 435–61.

Zhang, L; McMullen, BS; Valluri, D; Nakahara, K. *The Short- and Long-Run Impacts of Vehicle Mileage Fee on Income and Spatial Equity.* March 2009. https://wiki.umd.edu/lei/images/f/fe/Zhang2009b.pdf

## End Notes

[1] Schweitzer, L. and B. D. Taylor. "Just Pricing: The Distributional Effects of Congestion Pricing and Sales Taxes." Transportation, 35(6). 2008, pp. 797-812.

[2] The findings from the Literature Review are summarized in a report entitled Development of a Guidebook for State and Local Governments on Evaluating and Mitigating Equity Impacts of Road Pricing, Task 1 - Background Paper.

[3] The findings from the Workshop are summarized in a report entitled Development of a Guidebook for State and Local Governments on Evaluating and Mitigating Equity Impacts of Road Pricing, Task 2 – Summary Report on Workshop Findings.

[4] Parkany, Emily, "Environmental Justice Issues Related to Transponder Ownership and Road Pricing," Transportation Research Record, a Journal of the Transportation Research Board, No. 1932, 2005, pages 97-108.

[5] Adapted from Litman, T. (2002), "Evaluating Transportation Equity," World Transport Policy & Practice, Volume 8, No. 2, Summer 2002, pp. 50-65. Updated version available at: http://www.islandnet.com/~litman/equity.pdf.

[6] Based on Booz Allen project, Analysis of Federal Agency Practices in Implementing E.O. 12898 and Accompanying Presidential Memo, March 2011.

[7] FHWA and TxDOT, "Joint Guidance for Project and Network Level Environmental Justice, Regional Network Land Use, and Air Quality Analyses for Toll Roads," April 23, 2009. [Obtained by email between Anita Wilson and Patrick DeCorla-Souza, FHWA.]

[8] Ibid.

[9] Committee on the Equity of Transportation Finance Mechanisms, Equity of Evolving Transportation Finance Mechanisms, Transportation Research Board Special Report 303 (August 2011). http://onlinepubs.trb.org/onlinepubs/sr/sr303.pdf. Accessed Sept. 1, 2011.

[10] Weinstein, A., and G. C. Sciara, Assessing the Equity Implications of HOT Lanes: A Report Prepared for the Santa Clara Valley Transportation Authority (San Jose State University and University of California Berkeley, November 2004). http://www.vta.org/projects/hot_lanes/hot_equity.pdf. Accessed Sept. 1, 2011.

[11] FHWA and TxDOT, "Joint Guidance for Project and Network Level Environmental Justice, Regional Network Land Use, and Air Quality Analyses for Toll Roads," April 23, 2009. [Obtained by email between Anita Wilson and Patrick DeCorla-Souza, FHWA.]

[12] Plotnick, R., J. Romich, and J. Thacker. The Impacts of Tolling on Low-Income Persons in the Puget Sound Region. University of Washington, April 2009. http://www.wsdot.wa.gov/research/reports/fullreports/721.1.pdf. Accessed Sept. 1, 2011.

[13] Burris, M., and R. Hannay. "Equity Analysis of the Houston Quickride Project." Transportation Research Board Annual Meeting, March 2003.

[14] Goodwin, P. "The Rule of Three: A Possible Solution to the Political Problem of Competing Objectives for Road Pricing." Traffic Engineering and Control, Vol. 30, No. 10, 1989, pp. 495–97.

[15] Small, K., Using the Revenues from Congestion Pricing. Transportation, Vol. 19, No. 4, 1992, pp. 359-381.

[16] Committee on the Equity of Transportation Finance Mechanisms, Equity of Evolving Transportation Finance Mechanisms, Transportation Research Board Special Report 303 (August 2011). http://onlinepubs.trb.org/onlinepubs/sr/sr303.pdf Accessed Sept. 1, 2011.

[17] Litman T., Evaluating Transportation Equity, World Transport Policy & Practice, Vol. 8, No. 2, Summer 2002, pp. 50–65. Updated version (May 2011) available at http://www.islandnet.com/~litman/equity.pdf. Accessed Sept. 1, 2011.

[18] Bonsall, P., and C. Kelly. Road User Charging and Social Exclusion: The Impact of Congestion Charges on At-Risk Groups, Transport Policy, Vol. 12, No. 5, 2005, pp. 406–18.

[19] Schweitzer, L. and B. D. Taylor. Just Pricing: The Distributional Effects of Congestion Pricing and Sales Taxes. Transportation, 35(6). 2008, pp. 797-812.

[20] Committee on the Equity of Transportation Finance Mechanisms, Equity of Evolving Transportation Finance Mechanisms, Transportation Research Board Special Report 303 (August 2011 http://onlinepubs.trb.org/onlinepubs/sr/sr303.pdf. Accessed Sept. 1, 2011.

[21] Kockelman, K. M., and S. Kalmanje, Credit-Based Congestion Pricing: A Policy Proposal and the Public's Response, Transportation Research Part A: Policy and Practice, Vol. 39, No. 7–9, August–November 2005.

[22] DeCorla-Souza, P., Improving Metropolitan Transportation Efficiency with Fast Miles, Journal of Public Transportation, Vol. 9, No. 1, 2006, pp. 45–70.

[23] ICF International, Environmental Justice in Transportation: Emerging Trends and Best Practices. FHWA, 2011. http://www.fhwa.dot.gov/environment/ejustice/lib/guidebook/index.cfm. Accessed Sept. 1, 2011.

[24] FHWA, Income-Based Equity Impacts of Congestion Pricing: A Primer (FHWA Office of Transportation Management, 2009).

[25] DeCorla-Souza, P., Fair Highway Networks: A New Approach to Eliminate Congestion on Metropolitan Freeways, Public Works Management and Policy, Vol. 9, No. 3, 2005, pp. 196–205.

[26] Wear, B., Central Texas toll roads need more state subsidies than expected, The Statesman (July 18, 2011). http://www.statesman.com/news/local/central-texas-toll-roads-need-more-state-subsidies- 1618544.html. Accessed Sept. 1, 2011

[27] Bork, R., and M. Wrede, Political economy of commuting subsidies, Journal of Urban Economics No. 57, 2005, pp. 478–99.

[28] Toups, D. T., San Diego Association of Governments, "FasTrak Study—Follow-Up Questions," e-mail to Liisa Ecola, December 18, 2008.

[29] Leromonachou, P., S. Potter, and J. P. Warren, "Norway's Urban Toll Rings: Evolving Towards Congestion Charging?" Transport Policy, Vol. 13, No. 5, September 2006, pp. 367–78.

[30] Ecola L. and Light T., Equity and Congestion Pricing A Review of the Evidence (RAND 2009). http://www.rand.org/pubs/technical_reports/TR680.html. Accessed January 27, 2012.

[31] Committee on the Equity of Transportation Finance Mechanisms, Equity of Evolving Transportation Finance Mechanisms, Transportation Research Board Special Report 303 (August 2011). http://onlinepubs.trb.org/onlinepubs/sr/sr303.pdf. Accessed Sept. 1, 2011.

[32] Ecola L., and T. Light, Equity and Congestion Pricing A Review of the Evidence (RAND 2009). http://www.rand.org/pubs/technical_reports/TR680.html. Accessed Jan 27, 2012.

[33] Committee on the Equity of Transportation Finance Mechanisms, Equity of Evolving Transportation Finance Mechanisms, Transportation Research Board Special Report 303 (August 2011). http://onlinepubs.trb.org/onlinepubs/sr/sr303.pdf. Accessed Sept. 1, 2011.

[34] Ecola, L., and T. Light, Equity and Congestion Pricing A Review of the Evidence (RAND 2009). http://www.rand.org/pubs/technical_reports/TR680.html. Accessed Jan 27, 2012.

[35] Committee on the Equity of Transportation Finance Mechanisms. Equity of Evolving Transportation Finance Mechanisms, Transportation Research Board Special Report 303 (August 2011). http://onlinepubs.trb.org/onlinepubs/sr/sr303.pdf. Accessed Sept. 1, 2011.

[36] Equality of opportunity and equality of outcome are discussed further in Litman T., Evaluating Transportation Equity, World Transport Policy & Practice, Volume 8, No. 2, Summer 2002, pp. 50-65. Updated version (2011) available at http://www.islandnet.com/~litman/equity.pdf. Accessed Sept. 1, 2011.

[37] Ecola, L,. and T. Light, Equity and Congestion Pricing A Review of the Evidence (RAND 2009). http://www.rand.org/pubs/technical_reports/TR680.html. Accessed Jan. 27, 2011.

[38] Plotnick R., J. Romich, and J. Thacker, The Impacts of Tolling on Low-Income Persons in the Puget Sound Region (University of Washington, April 2009). http://www.wsdot.wa.gov/research/reports/fullreports/721.1.pdf. Accessed Sept. 1, 2011.

[39] Lam, T. C., and K. A. Small, The Value of Time and Reliability: Measurement from a Value Pricing Experiment, Transportation Research Part E, Vol. 37, No. 2–3, 2001, pp. 231–51.

[40] United States Code. Title VI: Nondiscrimination in Federally Assisted Programs, Civil Rights Act of 1964, 42 USC 2000(d) – 2000(d)(1).

[41] Committee on the Equity of Transportation Finance Mechanisms, Equity of Evolving Transportation Finance Mechanisms, Transportation Research Board Special Report 303 (August 2011). http://onlinepubs.trb.org/onlinepubs/sr/sr303.pdf. Accessed Sept. 1, 2011.

[42] Committee on the Equity of Transportation Finance Mechanisms, Equity of Evolving Transportation Finance Mechanisms, Transportation Research Board Special Report 303 (August 2011). http://onlinepubs.trb.org/onlinepubs/sr/sr303.pdf. Accessed Sept. 1, 2011.

[43] Ecola, L,. and T. Light, Equity and Congestion Pricing A Review of the Evidence (RAND 2009). http://www.rand.org/pubs/technical_reports/TR680.html. Accessed Jan . 27, 2012.

[44] Committee on the Equity of Transportation Finance Mechanisms, Equity of Evolving Transportation Finance Mechanisms, Transportation Research Board Special Report 303 (August 2011). http://onlinepubs.trb.org/onlinepubs/sr/sr303.pdf. Accessed Sept. 1, 2011.

[45] Committee on the Equity of Transportation Finance Mechanisms, Equity of Evolving Transportation Finance Mechanisms, Transportation Research Board Special Report 303 (August 2011). http://onlinepubs.trb.org/onlinepubs/sr/sr303.pdf. Accessed Sept. 1, 2011.

In: Potential Equity Impacts of Road Pricing
Editor: Raquel Boles
ISBN: 978-1-63117-111-6


*Chapter 2*

# INCOME-BASED EQUITY IMPACTS OF CONGESTION PRICING: A PRIMER*

***U.S. Department of Transportation***

## THE PURPOSE OF THIS VOLUME

This equity primer was produced to examine the impacts of congestion pricing on low-income groups, public opinion as expressed by various income groups, and ways to mitigate the equity impacts of congestion pricing.

* This is an edited, reformatted and augmented version of the U.S. Department of Transportation, Federal Highway Administration publication, FHWA-HOP-08-040, dated December 2008.

## INTRODUCTION

There are three principal types of equity considerations that relate to the distribution of benefits and burdens of toll or congestion-pricing projects:

1. *Income equity:* Are low-income groups negatively affected? Is a system that places the burden of travel-behavior change disproportionally on low- income individuals fair?
2. *Geographic equity:* Are some parts of the region made worse off than other parts? Will traffic diversion from tolled routes negatively impact neighborhoods or reduce performance on alternative toll-free routes?
3. *Modal equity:* Are public perceptions with regard to encouragement of multi-modal transportation addressed? For example, some believe that it is not fair to offer the same travel-time savings to those who pay a toll as to those who "do the right thing" by carpooling or taking transit.

This primer focuses on the first type of equity— income equity. Equity concerns with regard to income have often been raised about congestion pricing. The benefits of congestion pricing may not be distributed equally among all users. High-income users are more likely to remain on the highway, pay the congestion fee, and benefit from a faster trip. Low-income users may be worse off if they choose other less-expensive times, routes, or modes. When public use of infrastructure assets is deliberately made more expensive at certain times, low-income people and those concerned about their welfare may raise legitimate concerns about equity.

Toll roads impact environmental justice in at least two ways: impacts from the alignment and impacts from the ability to take advantage of better service. This primer focuses on the second impact—the ability to take advantage of better service—because the focus is on congestion pricing as applied to existing facilities. This primer presents information on the low-income equity issue in three sections as follows:

1. An overview of what is known about the low- income equity issue on the basis of current literature,
2. Results from studies conducted under the U.S. Department of Transportation's (DOT's) Value Pricing Pilot (VPP) Program, and
3. What is known about the issue, at this point in time, from DOT's urban partners funded under the Urban Partnership Agreement (UPA) Program and the Congestion Reduction Demonstration (CRD) Program.

The VPP Program was established by the U.S. Congress as the Congestion Pricing Pilot Program in 1991. It was subsequently renamed the VPP program under Section 1216 (a) of the Transportation Equity Act for the 21st Century (TEA-21) in 1998, and continued through the 2005 Safe, Accountable, Flexible, Efficient Transportation Equity Act: A Legacy for Users (SAFETEA-LU).

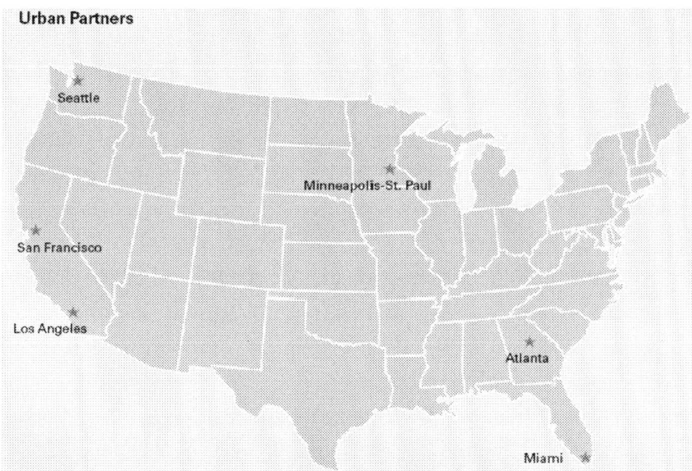


Map showing U.S. Department of Transportation urban partners under the Urban Partnership Agreement and Congestion Reduction Demonstration Programs.

The UPA Program was announced by U.S. DOT in May 2006 and was followed by the CRD Program, initiated in 2007. Both programs were designed to address congestion problems, with particular emphasis on establishing partnerships with major urban areas to make significant reductions in roadway congestion by using congestion pricing as a key strategy. There are currently six urban partner cities—Miami, FL; Atlanta, GA; Minneapolis, MN; Seattle, WA; San Francisco, CA; and Los Angeles, CA. New York, NY, was originally designated an urban partner but lost its urban partner status in April 2008 after it failed to obtain the legislative authority needed to implement congestion pricing.

## REVIEW OF THE LITERATURE

### Issues

The "fairness" question may be viewed within the context of the overall highway financing system, in which, in the absence of congestion fees, the costs of providing peak-period highway service are borne by all highway users, not just by those who travel during congested periods or on congested routes. In this context, placing more of the burden of paying for peak-period highway service on those who make use of peak highway capacity is being increasingly viewed as an equity improvement.

A well-designed value-pricing plan can be less burdensome to low-income citizens than current systems that are based on regressive taxes, such as car-registration fees, sales taxes, and the gas tax. For example, low-income drivers usually drive older vehicles that are not as fuel-efficient as newer models. They therefore must purchase more fuel per mile driven and consequently pay higher fuel taxes for each mile driven than do those who own newer fuel-efficient models.

A report by the U.S. Congressional Budget Office (1990) found that the tax on motor fuels was regressive relative to annual income. In addition, Schweitzer and Taylor (2008) noted in one study that most forms of transportation finance—fuel taxes, sales taxes, and tolls—are regressive forms of taxation in that they burden the poor more than they do the rich. Schweitzer and Taylor (2008) stated that, "Using sales taxes to fund roadways creates substantial savings to drivers by shifting some of the costs of driving from drivers to consumers at large, and in the process disproportionally favors the more affluent at the expense of the impoverished."

Another equity concern is that congestion pricing may make it too difficult or too expensive for low- skilled workers to get to their jobs. Entry-level and unskilled jobs are often not well served by public transit. Even if service routes exist for jobs of this type, the work hours for such jobs often require travel during off-peak service times, making public transit use less appealing as an option. Many low-skilled workers need to drive to retain their jobs; however, any congestion-pricing system can be sensitive to the issue of affordability, as discussed later in this primer.

When congestion pricing relies on an electronic cashless technology, households that do not have credit cards, bank accounts, or cannot afford large deposits may be unable to set up toll accounts, which may limit their use of these facilities. The Auto Express System in Puerto Rico mitigates many of these barriers by allowing users to purchase transponders and replenish their accounts by using cash at numerous retail and convenience stores without the need to provide a checking account or a credit card number. A light on the tag indicates when funds in the prepaid account are running low. Customers then have the option of replenishing their accounts at any number of locations, including gas stations. In Texas, TxTag accounts may be opened with cash. Those replenishing depleted accounts with cash must currently do so at a customer service center, but TxDOT is working with retailers to make TxTag services available at many retail outlets.

Another equity concern is that most tolled facilities that use electronic toll collection offer discounted tolls to those who use transponders rather than using video tolling or booth tolling. In situations in which the purchase of a transponder presents a significant economic barrier, low-income travelers who cannot afford a transponder will face a regressive toll schedule. It is estimated that between 10 and 20 percent of the population is unable to overcome these barriers to transponder ownership (Parkany, 2005).

## Impacts on Low-Income Groups

Congestion-priced facilities currently in operation in the United States include tollways and tolled water crossings with variable tolls and priced lanes along major transportation corridors that experience high levels of congestion (U.S. DOT, 2008). Such congestion-pricing projects are operating in California, Minnesota, Washington, Colorado, Utah, Florida, Texas, New Jersey, and New York. The data from priced lanes have shown that a wide range of income groups use the lanes at different levels of frequency of use.

The use of congestion-priced lanes by both high- and low-income users appears to be selective. If use of priced facilities was solely dependent on income, then low-income travelers would never use such facilities. Studies have indicated that roughly half of the users of congestion-priced lanes do so once a week or less. Weinstein and Sciara (2004) suggested that the impacts of congestion pricing are not necessarily related to income and can also be based on flexibility of time and routes available to users.

**Commuting pattern by income group in the Portland, OR, area**

| | Less Than Poverty Guideline | 100%-200% of Poverty Guideline | More Than 400% of Poverty Guideline |
|---|---|---|---|
| Not Employed | 58.7% | 43.2% | 16.7% |
| SOV-Peak | 17.1% | 14.6% | 35.4% |
| SOV-Off-Peak | 4.3% | 13.4% | 19.2% |
| Carpool-Peak | 5.7% | 7.2% | 9.8% |
| Carpool-Off-Peak | 5.7% | 2.3% | 2.2% |
| All Other Modes | 8.5% | 19.2% | 16.6% |
| Total | 100.0% | 100.0% | 100.0% |
| Number of Cases | 109 | 229 | 575 |
| Missing Cases* | (16) | (21) | (63) |

* Missing data concerning mode of travel were allocated proportionately across five commuter categories.

SOV = single-occupancy vehicle.

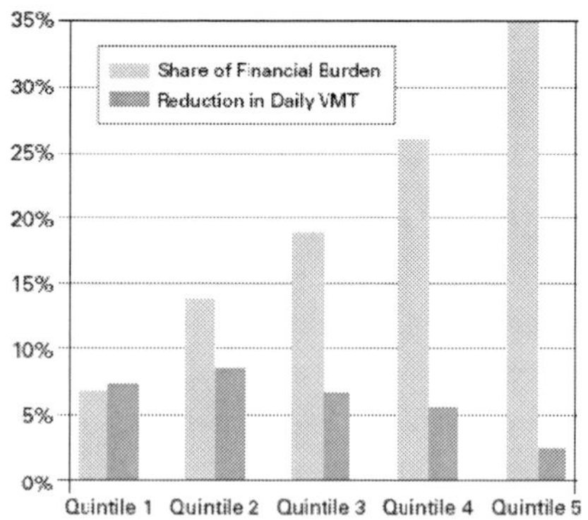


Equity implications of hypothetical Los Angeles 5-cent vehicle-miles-traveled (VMT) fee, 1991.

A paper by the Rand Corporation and Volpe National Transportation Systems Center (2007) indicated that household surveys suggest that rush-hour travelers who travel in the busier direction—and thus are more likely to pay congestion charges—are the most affluent group within the larger category of street and highway users.

Congestion pricing clearly will create economic hardship for some households. Svadlenak and Jones (1998) found that of adult residents in the Portland, OR, area who travel during peak hours in single- occupant vehicles, approximately 3 percent are low-income commuters. Of all Portland-area commuters, 38 percent travel during peak hours in single-occupant vehicles and have relatively high incomes. Svadlenak and Jones (1998) suggested that of this 38 percent, most can afford tolls and would welcome tolls if they resulted in a commensurate improvement in travel time.

Deakin and Harvey (1996) found that, if a 5-cent vehicle-miles-traveled fee were to be imposed in Los Angeles, CA, the lowest income quintile (i.e., 20 percent of users) would bear only 7 percent of the financial burden, whereas the highest income quintile would bear 35 percent of the financial burden.

Safirova et al. (2003) estimated the impacts of a high-occupancy toll (HOT) lane network in the Washington, DC, area. They found that the lowest income quartile would pay 5.2 percent of tolls, whereas the highest income quartile would pay 50.3 percent of tolls.

**Welfare changes and equity impacts by income group under high-occupancy-toll (HOT) lane network policy in the Washington, DC, area**

| Quartile | Tolls paid by income group ($000/year) | Percentage of tolls paid by income group | Welfare change* ($000/ year) | Percentage of welfare change accruing to quartile | Welfare change as percentage of income |
|---|---|---|---|---|---|
| 1 | 3,412 | 5.2 | 3,047 | 2.9 | 0.028 |
| 2 | 7,822 | 12.0 | 12,172 | 11.5 | 0.037 |
| 3 | 21,073 | 32.4 | 32,717 | 30.9 | 0.050 |
| 4 | 32,728 | 50.3 | 57,935 | 54.7 | 0.042 |
| Total | 65,035 | 100.0 | 105,870 | 100.0 | 0.045 |

*Before counting the value of toll revenues.

Source: Welfare and Distributional Effects of Road Pricing Schemes for Metropolitan Washington, DC. Elena Safirova, Kenneth Gillingham, Ian Parry, Peter Nelson, Winston Harrington, and David Mason, October 2003—Discussion Paper 03-57.

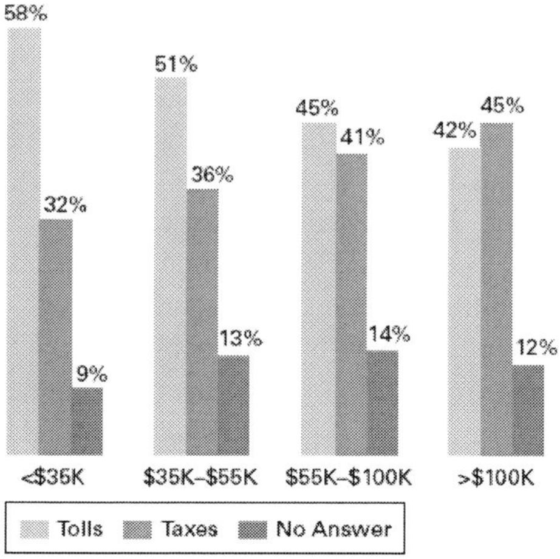


Support for tolls versus taxes in King County, Washington. Low-income households prefer tolls over taxes.

Transek (2006) found that, in the case of the Stockholm city center congestion-pricing scheme, affluent men in the inner city pay the most in congestion-pricing charges. Because high-income individuals use their cars more frequently, it was found that high-income households were more likely to incur the congestion charge compared with the average household. This analysis indicates that, if the revenues are used for public transportation, those who gain the most from the pricing scheme are young people, low-income individuals, single people, women, and residents of the inner suburbs. These groups pay relatively little in congestion charges on average and use public transportation more often than do other groups.

## Public Opinion

Taniguchi (2008) provided results from a survey of public opinion on paying for transportation infrastructure with tolls versus taxes. The survey found that support for tolls was higher among low-income individuals (58 percent support for tolls) than among high-income individuals (42 percent support for tolls). Support for taxes was 32 percent for low-income individuals compared with 45 percent for high-income individuals.

Morallos (2006) found that, although limited, evidence from the successfully operating VPP projects clearly demonstrates that the most valued feature in tolling and pricing projects is that of providing people with a choice of whether to use priced lanes. Studies have shown that lower income individuals face the greatest financial harm when they are denied adequate travel choices. Lack of choice to pay a toll in exchange for reliable travel times can result in lost wages or late fees for daycare that could have been avoided.

Even when priced lanes are seen to be used more heavily by high-income users than by low-income users, a broad spectrum of income groups still express approval of the projects (as documented later in this primer) because they are given the choice of choosing the tolled route, an alternative free route, or a different transportation mode. Although high- income motorists do use the priced lanes more often, all income groups value the choice of a reliable trip travel time that is now available to them, serving their needs when they absolutely have to get to their destinations on time (e.g., getting to a daycare center before late fees kick in).

## Addressing Equity Concerns

Research has identified strategies for addressing equity concerns through redistribution of toll revenues. These include distributing rebates or credits, or revenue transfer to transit and carpooling services in the priced corridor. To ensure that at least some surplus toll revenue is used to improve transit, some areas have passed legislation to dedicate a portion of the surplus revenue to transit, whereas others have created special transit accounts.

A particularly important consideration in evaluating congestion-pricing options and their equity implications is the use of revenues generated by tolls. Toll revenues can be used to compensate those who might otherwise consider themselves “losers” as a result of congestion pricing. Compensation can come in a variety of forms. Toll revenues may be used to finance highway improvements (particularly in the corridor where the tolls are levied) or to pay for improvements in transit service. In cases in which effects on low-income drivers are felt to be particularly severe, toll exemptions or toll rebates may be offered to eligible drivers, or other forms of monetary compensation may be offered, such as tax rebates that provide reimbursement for tolls paid or income supplements.

Each of these approaches has been used or considered for use in congestion-pricing programs. For example, revenues from area pricing in Central London were used in part to improve bus service into the priced area, thereby enhancing transportation services to low-income groups and other users of those systems. The statutes in California mandate that 18 percent of toll revenues from the Bay Area Toll Authority be transferred into three accounts controlled by the Metropolitan Transportation Commission, a multimodal planning agency for the region. The Port Authority of New York and New Jersey likewise uses surplus toll revenue to subsidize transit services. When New York City considered a cordon-pricing scheme, it proposed a tax rebate for drivers who qualified for the federal-earned income tax credit. In the case of a proposed congestion-pricing scheme on the San Francisco Bay Bridge, tolls were to be raised from $1 to $3 per trip, but the proposal called for a reduced "lifeline" toll rate of $1 for low-income users.

Schweitzer and Taylor (2008) suggested that if policymakers are worried about low-income, peak- period commuters paying tolls, one way to address this would be to provide discounted "lifeline" pricing based on income levels, as is done by utility companies for qualifying customers. As an alternative, they could provide travel credits to low-income commuters.

## Evidence from VPP Program Projects

The perception that value pricing is "unfair" to low- and perhaps even middle-income drivers has been a concern for many VPP program projects. Since the inception of the VPP program, equity has been a key issue of interest, with particular attention given to mitigating possible adverse effects of projects on low-income drivers. Project experiences are summarized in FHWA's report on lessons learned from the program (KT Analytics and Cambridge Systematics, Inc., 2008). Project experience has shown, particularly for the most common projects funded under the early phases of the program (e.g., HOT lanes), that the perception of unfairness may be exaggerated. Data from the various cities that have implemented projects or have projects underway are discussed below. Most of the data have been obtained from projects involving "partial" pricing on one or more lanes of a freeway facility. Equity impacts relating to income have not been evaluated in the case of "full facility" pricing projects, such as those implemented on tollways and tolled water crossings. Overall, the perception that congestion pricing is an inequitable way of responding to the problem of traffic congestion does not appear to be borne out by experience.

## Experience from "Partial" Pricing Projects

### *San Diego, CA*

For the I-15 HOT lanes in San Diego, CA, user and stakeholder concerns about the potential elitist character of the project arose in the first year but diminished with time as users across income groups used the facility. By the final evaluation, such concerns were minimal. In the case of the planned expansion and extension of the I-15 HOT lanes, a telephone survey of all facility users of I-15 found that most consider the extension fair to regular-lane users (71 percent approval) and to HOT-lane users (75 percent approval). There were very few differences in attitudes about the fairness of the lanes based on ethnicity or income; however, half of respondents felt that tolling solo drivers was an unfair double taxation. HOT-lane users paying tolls were less likely to feel that way than were other corridor users.

When considering the statement, "People who drive alone should be able to use the I-15 express lanes for a fee," 80 percent of the lowest income motorists using the I-15 corridor agreed with it, and for value-pricing concepts, which are viewed as "buying time" for a premium level of service. low-income users were more likely to support the statement than were the highest income users.

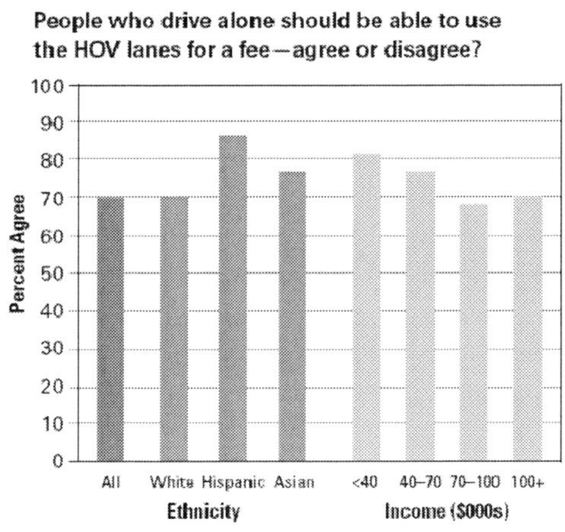


Public acceptance of I-15 high-occupancy toll lanes by income group and ethnicity. There is wide support for value-pricing concepts, which are viewed as "buying time" for a premium level of service.

Users of San Diego's I-15 HOT lanes were more likely to have higher incomes than were drivers in regular lanes, but lower income drivers sometimes did use the HOT lanes. I-15 drivers showed a broad approval of the HOT-lane program and felt that it was fair and had reduced congestion. Equity issues are addressed by dedicating the HOT-lane revenues to bus service in the corridor. I-15 was the first project to demonstrate that implementing tolls as a demand-management measure can play a major role in paying for transit and reducing the negative impact of this strategy on low-income individuals.

***Denver, CO***

For the I-25/US-36 HOT lanes in Denver, CO, public outreach leading to implementation of HOT lanes did not uncover critical concerns regarding equity or other social impacts, nor have such concerns arisen since implementation.

***Minneapolis, MN***

On I-394 in Minneapolis, MN, the first attempt at implementing HOT lanes in1 997 met resistance in large part because of public belief that only high- income users would benefit. A second attempt approximately 9 years later succeeded in part because advocates made the case that all income groups value time savings and reliability for certain trips. Worsening congestion and a shortage of transportation funds were also important to the success of the second attempt, according to evaluators. Surveys of corridor users found a relatively small difference in income between those who do and those who do not own transponders: 25 percent of owners had annual incomes of $50,000 or less compared with 32 percent of non-owners. However, concerns about equity have not been significant since start up.

Patterson and Levinson (2008) stated that "the [HOT] lanes are Lexus Lanes in the sense that increased income predicts increases in three of the four metrics used to measure direct benefit.... Individuals with higher incomes receive more direct benefits from the lane than those with lower incomes." However, according to the University of Minnesota and NuStats (2005), HOT-lane usage with MnPass was reported across all income levels, including by 79 percent of high-income respondents, 70 percent of middle-income respondents, and 55 percent of low-income respondents.

Patterson and Levinson (2008) sought to determine whether the higher levels of MnPass use found among wealthier drivers was attributable to their residential location (specifically along the managed- lanes corridor) or to their income. Both factors were found to be significant. The highest income motorists paid the most (in average and total tolls) and received the most benefit.

Patterson and Levinson (2008) cited specific equity benefits of managed lanes:

- Vehicle shifts away from general-purpose lanes lead to improved travel conditions on such lanes,
- A high-quality transit alternative is generally part of a managed-lanes project,
- Unused transponders may be considered to provide high-value travel-time insurance to their owners, and
- When social benefits are paid for by those who choose to drive, situational equity is generally improved.

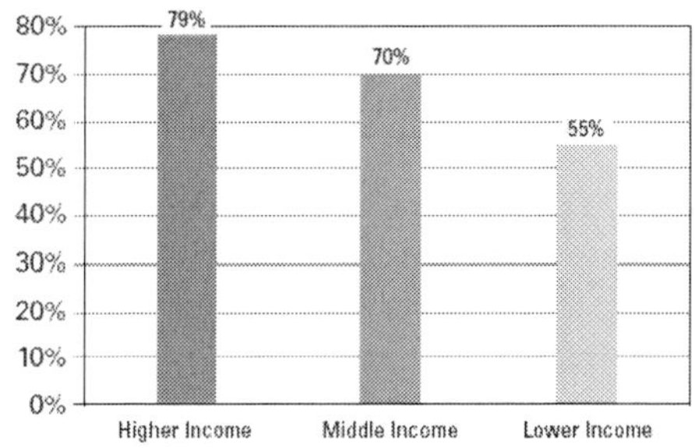


Users of I-394 MnPass high-occupancy toll lanes as a percentage of Minneapolis, MN, population.

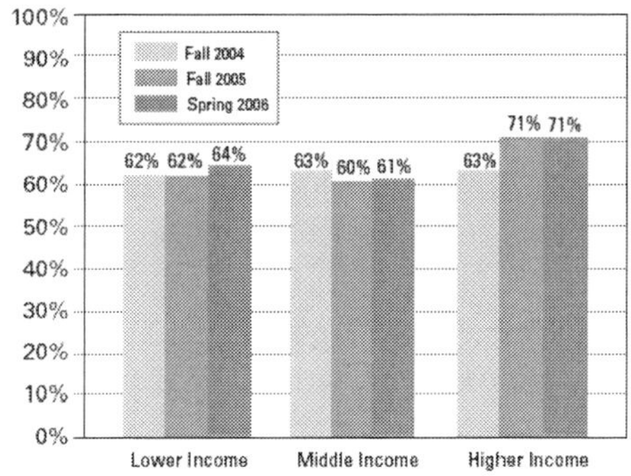


Percentage of Minneapolis consumers surveyed who approve of allowing single-occupant drivers to use the carpool lane for a fee.

Approximately 65 percent of respondents to a survey conducted in spring 2006, a year after initial implementation, thought that HOT lanes were a good idea. Support for the lanes was also found to be high across income levels, including by 71 percent of high-income respondents, 61 percent of middle-income respondents, and 64 percent of low- income respondents.

### *Houston, TX*

For the I-10 and US-290 HOT lanes in Houston, TX, focus groups held during project planning did not find concerns about social equity among either corridor users or the public at large. The general reaction was that all would benefit if congestion were reduced. There also have been no equity concerns raised during operations. It should be noted, however, that these HOT lanes are somewhat different from other examples, that is, single-occupant vehicles are not permitted in the HOT lanes—tolls are used to manage two-person carpool demand. Burris et al. (2007) found that even in the lowest income group, over two-thirds of respondents were interested in paying to use the HOT lanes.

### *Seattle, WA*

For SR-1 67 HOT lanes in Seattle, WA, evaluators found through outreach efforts that low-income drivers are as supportive of the HOT lanes as are drivers from other income groups.

### *Orange County, CA*

SR-91 in Orange County, CA, was the first project to implement congestion pricing on new lanes and until 2008 was the only operating example of congestion pricing on new lanes. FHWA's *A Guide for HOT Lane Development* report (FHWA, 2005) provides data from studies of SR-9 1 express toll lanes in California. At any given time, about one-quarter of the vehicles in toll lanes are driven by high-income individuals, whereas the remaining cars are driven by low- and middle-income individuals. It is estimated that 19 percent of the peak-period users of the SR-9 1 express lanes make less than $40,000 a year, and 42 percent make less than $60,000 a year. Low-income drivers do use the express lanes and are as likely to approve of the lanes as drivers with higher incomes. In fact, over half of commuters with household incomes less than $25,000 a year approved of providing toll lanes.

An evaluation of the SR-91 express lanes (Sullivan, 2000) found a "moderate" income effect, with the percentage of trips on the express lanes for the lowest and highest income groups (20 percent and 50 percent) staying the same over the 3-year evaluation period. Evaluators also found that the use of express lanes increased over time for both those who carpooled and solo drivers across all incomes. Low-income and moderate-income travelers appeared to be more selective and used the tolled route for less than half of their trips.

When prices rose, people in the lowest income group did not reduce their travel, but people of moderate income did. This suggests that people with lower incomes have less flexibility in the time they travel (Kuehn, 2008), or that low-income individuals have very high values for reliable travel when they need it.

## Experience from "Full Facility" Pricing Projects

### *Lee County, FL*

In Florida, proposals to raise peak-period tolls on Lee County's bridges were rejected as inequitable to those with inflexible schedules and led to a program of reduced off-peak tolls instead. Income equity was not raised as an issue in planning or in evaluation focus groups and surveys.

### *New York, NY*

The Port Authority of New York and New Jersey did not uncover major equity issues in planning for variable tolls, nor did they evaluate equity effects after program implementation.

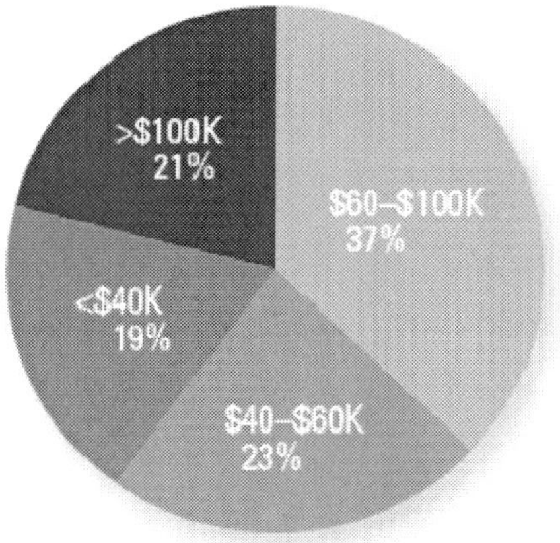


Annual household income of SR-91 peak-period travelers in 1999.

## Planning Studies Conducted Under The VPP Program

Studies funded under the VPP program have included innovative approaches designed specifically to address equity issues. The authors of one study evaluated the equity impacts of a regional value pricing program, which are discussed below.

### *Fast and Intertwined Regular (FAIR) Lanes*

This approach was studied in Alameda County, CA, and involved providing toll credits to qualified low- income users on the basis of their monitored usage of free regular lanes located adjacent to HOT lanes. Accumulated credits allowed for periodic free use of the HOT lanes by these motorists.

### *"FAST Miles"*

The FAST Miles approach being studied in Minneapolis would allocate a fixed amount of toll credits to all area motorists, similar to the limited number of free peak-period minutes allocated by cell phone companies to their customers. Total credits allocated to all motorists would be limited by the peak-period capacity available on the roadway system. This would ensure that demand would not exceed supply of road space (i.e., roadway capacity) and guarantee congestion-free travel for all motorists in exchange for use of their free credits to "pay" for roadway use.

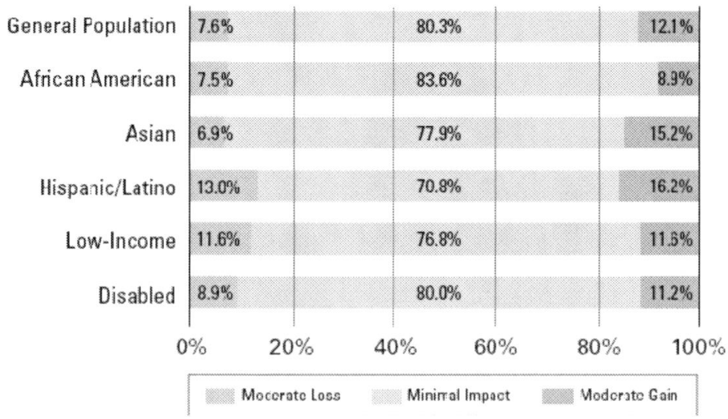


Demographic assessment of the change in accessibility to jobs by highways.

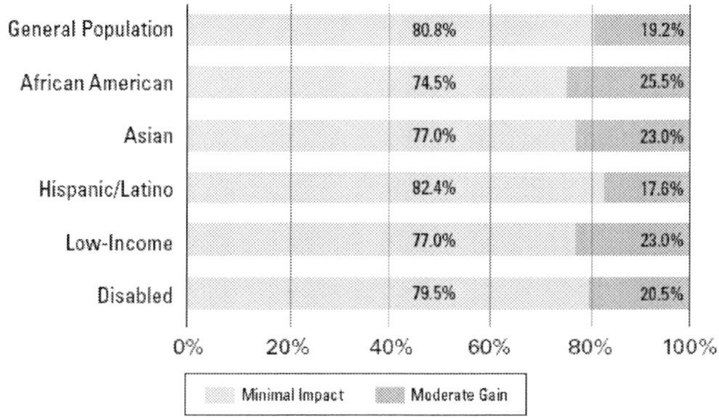


Demographic assessment of the change in accessibility to jobs by transit.

***Network of Variably Priced Lanes in the Washington, DC, Metropolitan Area***

An analysis was performed for three scenarios involving a network of priced lanes (National Capital Region Transportation Planning Board, 2008). With respect to transit, because transit service was added between the base case and the scenarios, only gains in accessibility were noted. With regard to highways, one scenario had no losses in accessibility; thus, no population group experienced losses. The pattern of losses and gains for the other two scenarios were very similar, with no one population group receiving a large share of the benefit and no one population group shouldering a disproportionate share of the losses. Gains and losses in accessibility to jobs by highways across population groups for one scenario is presented in the figure "Demographic assessment of the change in accessibility to jobs by highways," and the distribution of gains in accessibility to jobs by transit for the same scenario is presented in the figure "Demographic assessment of the change in accessibility to jobs by transit."

## EQUITY IMPLICATIONS OF URBAN PARTNERSHIP AGREEMENTS

FHWA conducted a survey of the UPA cities (including New York) to gather information about the real and perceived equity implications of their projects. In addition to equity by income, regional geographic equity was also considered in some instances, because the costs of congestion pricing and the distribution of benefits (typically in the form of new transit and ferry services funded from toll revenue) may be distributed unequally, as with any transportation policy that does not involve tolls or pricing. The comprehensive evaluations that take place in the UPA cities will each, to some degree, provide further examination of equity issues after the projects are in operation. Details about the projects are available on FHWA's Web site at http://www.upa.dot.gov/index.htm

## Miami, FL

Focus groups were conducted in 1995 in regard to South Florida's managed lanes on I-95. The focus groups discussed potential traffic-improvement strategies, including managed lanes. Of the nine focus groups of approximately 10 participants each, five were conducted in English, three in Spanish, and one in Creole. Although focus groups by their nature do not present a statistically valid representation of public opinion, their results may nevertheless be indicative of such opinion. Focus groups also have the benefit of ensuring that people fully understand the aspects of an issue before voicing their opinions.

A key finding from the focus groups is that the perceptions of benefits from managed lanes did not divide along any apparent demographic boundary, including ethnicity and income. The managed-lanes concept was found to be difficult to communicate, but after sufficient time was taken to convey the concept clearly, participants generally perceived that both personal and regional benefits would result from managed-lanes implementation. As could be expected, participants said that they would use managed lanes less frequently as the price to use these lanes rises. It is interesting to note, however, that many individuals had been unaware of toll increases that took place in the region shortly before the focus groups were conducted, suggesting that those who participated in the focus groups might be overestimating their price sensitivity.

## San Francisco, CA

A 2007 survey asked 600 residents of the San Francisco, CA, region (JD Franz Research, Inc., 2007) about support for studying congestion pricing. Support was found to be slightly higher among very- low- and low-income residents of the region relative to other residents. San Francisco's UPA project managers offered a theory for this result: Lower income residents are more likely to be transit riders who would benefit from both reduced congestion and increased transit investments from pricing revenues. For low-income drivers, their increased likelihood of having less scheduling flexibility (e.g., due to having to punch a time clock) and concern about daycare late fees may cause them to more highly value reduced congestion and greater travel time reliability.

## Seattle, WA

King County, WA, conducted a transportation survey in December 2007 (EMC Research Inc., 2007). Many questions were asked of the 501 respondents, a number of them pertaining to support for tolling. Although the survey report did indicate the percentage of respondents in each income group, survey responses were not broken out by income. Among the findings was high support for tolling when compared with other alternatives when a specific infrastructure need was presented. Between 78 and 84 percent (depending on the order in which answers were presented) of respondents preferred electronic tolls over a sales tax increase to fund the SR 520 bridge replacement.

Support for tolling grew substantially if a portion of revenues was dedicated to transit, even if tolls had to be significantly higher to allow for such a diversion of revenue to occur. A toll of $2.50 to fund the replacement of the Lake Washington floating bridge was supported by 64 percent of respondents, whereas 74 percent supported a $4 toll to fund the bridge replacement along with increased transit and bicycling investments in the corridor. Thus, the equity and other benefits of improved transportation options were shown to be more important to respondents than was keeping the toll rates as low as possible.

With revenues dedicated to replacing the SR 520 bridge, 69 percent of respondents indicated support for variable tolling. In regard to another roadway, in which the need for tolling revenues was not presented, only 28 percent of survey participants indicated support for variable tolling, even after the benefits of such tolling in terms of relieving congestion were described to them. The bottom line is that the use of revenues is an extremely important determinant of public support for congestion pricing and is likely to be a more important determinant of support than the level of congestion charges and the design of the congestion-pricing scheme.

## New York, NY

An analysis was conducted for the New York City Traffic Congestion Mitigation Commission with regard to the regional equity implications of three cordon pricing and tolling scenarios and supporting transit services (New York City Traffic Congestion Mitigation Commission, 2008). Results from the analysis are discussed below.

### *Geographic Equity*

The analysis of the regional equity implications of the scenarios under consideration started by emphasizing the regional inequities from existing toll policies, in which 45 percent of toll revenues collected from drivers bound for Manhattan's central business district (CBD) are paid by New Jersey residents, even though New Jersey vehicles constitute only 24 percent of the total drivers heading into the CBD. This 45 percent figure can be compared with Manhattan drivers, who currently pay only 7 percent of collected toll revenues, and residents of the other four boroughs of New York City, who pay a total of 29 percent.

Three scenarios were considered: (1) the mayor's cordon pricing plan, (2) an alternative modified cordon pricing plan, and (3) tolling of existing free bridges into Manhattan. For new tolls under the various scenarios, Manhattan residents would pay between 28 and 31 percent, residents of the other four boroughs would pay between 38 and 49 percent, and New Jersey residents would pay only an additional 7 to 17 percent. The new toll revenues would be dedicated to subsidizing transit, and the new transit would primarily serve New York City residents. The new bus routes would be along the corridors where there is substantial car commuting, further relieving congestion along these routes and thus directly benefiting those who continue to commute by car.

The analysis concluded that between 22 and 24 percent of revenues for the transit subsidies would come from Manhattan drivers, and 41 percent would come from drivers from other boroughs, which would appear to be fair. Both the mayor's congestion-pricing plan and the alternative congestion-pricing plan were found to "allocate transit subsidies among drivers largely in proportion to the percentage of CBD-bound drivers in each geographic area." The toll plan, which added tolls to bridges that are currently toll-free, "allocates transit subsidies less proportionately as compared to the two congestion pricing plans."

***Income Equity***

Councilwoman Melissa Mark-Viverito's blog posting on January 30, 2008 (Mark-Viverito, 2008), partially excerpted on this page, speaks for itself.

The New York City mayor's proposed congestion-pricing plan, the alternative congestion-pricing plan, and the toll plan all included the imposition of new fees and tolls. To better understand the impacts of these costs on different socioeconomic groups, agency staff examined the income profiles of those groups most likely to pay the fee or toll. This analysis raised several issues for further consideration, as discussed below.

The fee and toll plans most impact those who drive to the CBD on a daily basis; the vast majority of trips into the zone are not made by automobile. Therefore, individuals who typically walk, bike, or take transit to the CBD would not be financially affected by the fee or toll options. Of motorists, those who drive into the CBD every day for work would be most impacted. For example, under the mayor's plan, a daily auto commuter who travels from Upper Manhattan to the Financial District would pay about $2,000 in congestion fees each year (vs. $912 a year for those who use transit). By comparison, a motorist who drives into the zone on weekdays once or twice a month for shopping or entertainment would pay about $100 to $200 a year in congestion fees under the mayor's plan.

Those who commute by car to the CBD earn comparatively higher incomes: New York City DOT staff analyzed the income levels of city and suburban residents who use the automobile as their primary mode to reach Manhattan jobs. Staff found that of the 2.14 million workers in Manhattan, about 292,000, or 14 percent, drive to work each day. These workers have a median annual income of $60,941, compared with a median annual income of $46,416 for all workers in Manhattan, including the 1.85 million workers who take transit, walk, or bike to work. In aggregate, the fee would most impact commuters who earn 31 percent more than the median income of all Manhattan workers. Taking into account other income earners in the household, workers who drive to work in Manhattan have a median household income of $103,700. This compares with a median household income of $89,379 for all Manhattan workers.

A small proportion of low- and moderate-income commuters who drive would be disproportionately impacted by a fee or toll: Most low- and moderate-income commuters who travel into the CBD take transit or walk and would not be impacted by a fee or toll. Of all New York City residents who commute to work, only 5 percent drive to the CBD. Of that 5 percent, most (80 percent) have a feasible transit alternative to get to work that would take no more than 15 minutes longer than their auto trip. Therefore, only 1 percent of Manhattan workers lack a viable alternative to paying a congestion fee or toll. The low- and moderate-income workers disproportionately impacted by a fee or a toll represent a further subgroup within this 1 percent. Legislation that was proposed for consideration by the State legislature would have provided tax credits to compensate low-income motorists for amounts that they would have to pay in excess of the round-trip transit fare.

> "In the East Harlem and South Bronx communities that I represent, we are automatically skeptical when business interests and politicians from outside our communities claim to be watching out for us— because nine times out of 10, they're doing just the opposite.
>
> " So it is with congestion pricing. For months, some suburban elected officials from wealthy areas, as well as a coalition backed primarily by the American Automobile Association and Manhattan garage owners, have tried their best to cloak themselves as guardians of New York's poor and middle-class residents.
>
> " ...The truth is that just 5 percent of commuters in Brooklyn, Queens, Staten Island and the Bronx travel to Manhattan by private car. People who drive their cars to work also earn 30 percent more a year than those of us who use mass transit. It is our poor and middle-class families who would benefit from congestion pricing—as the fees charged to drivers would be used to improve the bus and subway system.
>
> " Critics have also tried to whitewash congestion pricing's health benefits to communities such as Harlem and the Bronx, where kids are hospitalized for asthma attacks far more often than in Westchester, Nassau and Suffolk counties...
>
> " Unlike those who falsely claim to speak for the best interests of my constituents, the commission ought to recognize it would be irresponsible not to pursue a policy that could provide immediate and measurable relief of traffic congestion while improving the air that all of my constituents breathe and the buses and subways that they ride daily."
>
> Councilwoman Melissa Mark-Viverito's blog posting on January 30, 2008.

A large number of low- and moderate-income residents would benefit from improved transit services under any of the three revenue-generating plans: As a group, low- and moderate-income New York City residents rely more on transit for their travel needs when compared with higher income residents. Therefore, these low- and moderate-income residents would benefit more from the short- term transit enhancements that would precede a toll or fee imposition and from the expansion of the transit system made possible by increased revenues for transit investment.

## CONCLUSION

Any change in the way charges are made for road use will benefit some individuals more than others. Those who have higher incomes will tend to use congestion-priced facilities more often, which leads to a perception that wealthy people are favored; however, income-related equity concerns may not be entirely warranted. Although data from priced lanes that are operated in the United States show that high-income motorists do use the lanes more often, the lanes are used by all income groups, serving drivers' needs when they absolutely have to get to their destinations on time (e.g., getting to a daycare center before late fees kick in). Moreover, approval ratings are equally high for all income groups, in the 60–80 percent range, because all income groups value the "insurance" of a reliable trip time when they absolutely need it.

Low-income travelers who take transit more frequently will benefit from transit-service improvements that generally accompany congestion pricing. Toll revenues can be used to compensate those who might otherwise consider themselves "losers" as a result of congestion pricing. Low-income transit riders can benefit significantly from toll-financed transit improvements, which are generally included in any pricing package. In cases in which effects on low-income drivers are perceived to be particularly severe, such drivers could be provided with toll exemptions, rebates, or other forms of monetary compensation, such as tax rebates or income supplements. Pricing schemes may include protections for low-income individuals, such as toll credits.

## REFERENCES


[1] Burris, M., Sadabadi, K. F., Mattingly, S. P., Mahlawat, M., Li, J., Rasmidatta, I. & Saroosh, A. (2007). Reaction to the managed lane concept by various groups of travelers. *Transportation Research Record: Journal of the Transportation Research Board,* 1996, 74–82.

[2] Deakin, E. & Harvey, G. (1996, November). *Transportation pricing strategies for California: An assessment of congestion, energy and equity impacts.* Sacramento: California Air Resources Board.

[3] EMC Research, Inc. (2007, December 15–20). *King County transportation survey.* (Conducted on behalf of the King County Department of Transportation.) Retrieved February 9, 2009, from http://www.metrokc.gov/exec/news/2008/pdf/3798apx.pdf

[4] Federal Highway Administration. (2005). *A guide for HOT lane development.* Retrieved February 9, 2009, from http://www.its.dot.gov/JPODOCS/REPTS_TE/13668_files/images/13668.pdf

[5] Hubert H. Humphrey Institute, University of Minnesota, & NuStats. (2006). *Panel survey for MnPASS HOT lanes evaluation.* Retrieved February 9, 2009, from http://ganymede.nustats.com/nustats_dot_com/templates/yet_again_new-menu/docs/case_studies/panel_surveyjor_mnpass_hotJanes.pdf

[6] JD Franz Research, Inc. (2007 August). *Poll about congestion pricing.* (Conducted on behalf of the San Francisco County Transportation Authority.)

[7] KT Analytics, Inc. & Cambridge Systematics, Inc. (2008). *Value pricing pilot program: Lessons learned.* (Prepared for the Federal Highway Administration.) Retrieved February 9, 2009, from http://ops.fhwa.dot.gov/publications/fhwahop08023/vpppJessonslearned.pdf

[8] Kuehn, D. (2008). *Environmental justice and the distribution of benefits from highway pricing programs.* Paper presented on behalf of the Federal Highway Administration at the 2009 Annual Meeting of the Transportation Research Board, Washington, DC.

[9] Mark-Viverito, M. (2008, January 30). Voices: Congestion pricing fairest for the poor. *New York Metro Newspaper.*

[10] Morallos, D. (2006, August). *Social equity issues with tolling and pricing.* Unpublished manuscript, Summer Transportation Internship Program for Diverse Groups, Federal Highway Administration, Washington, DC.

[11] National Capital Region Transportation Planning Board. (2008, February). *Evaluating alternative scenarios for a network of variably priced highway lanes in the metropolitan Washington region.* Retrieved February 11, 2009, from http://www.mwcog.org/TPB/VPTF/docs/RVPS_Final_Report.pdf

[12] New York City Traffic Congestion Mitigation Commission. (2008, January). *Report to the Traffic Congestion Mitigation Commission and recommended implementation plan.* Retrieved February 11, 2009, from https://www.nysdot.gov/portal/page/portal/programs/congestion_mitigation_commission/final-recommendation

[13] Parkany, E. (2005, January). *Environmental justice issues related to transponder ownership and road pricing* (No. 05-2274). Paper presented at the 84th Annual Meeting of the Transportation Research Board, Washington, DC.

[14] Patterson, T. M. & Levinson, D. (2008, March). *Lexus lanes or Corolla lanes? Spatial use and equity patterns on the I-394 MnPASS lanes.* Unpublished manuscript, Department of Civil Engineering, University of Minnesota. Retrieved February 11, 2009, from http://nexus.umn.edu/Papers/MnPASSEquity.pdf

[15] Rand Corporation & Volpe National Transportation Systems Center. (2007, January 31). *Congestion pricing: Revenue potential* (Commission briefing paper 5A-08). Prepared for the Section 1909 Commission, U.S. Department of Transportation, Washington, DC.

[16] Safirova, E., Gillingham, K., Parry, I., Nelson, P., Harrington, W. & Mason, D. (2003, October). *Welfare and distributional effects of road pricing schemes for metropolitan Washington DC* (Discussion paper 03-57). Resources for the Future, Washington, DC.

[17] Schweitzer, L. & Taylor, B. (2008, November). Just pricing: The distributional effects of congestion pricing and sales taxes. *Transportation, 35*, (6), 797–812.

[18] Sullivan, E. (2000, December). *Continuation study to evaluate the impacts of the SR 91 value-priced express lanes.* Cal Poly State University, San Luis Obispo, CA. Retrieved February 11, 2009, from http://ceenve3.civeng.calpoly.edu/sullivan/SR91/final_rpt/FinalRep2000.pdf

[19] Svadlenak, J. & Jones, B. (1998). Congestion pricing and ability to pay: Income levels and poverty rates of peak-hour, single-occupant vehicle commuters in Portland, Oregon. *Northwest Journal of Business and Economics.*

[20] Taniguchi, H. S. (2008). *Tolling in Washington state.* King County Department of Transportation, Washington. Presentation retrieved February 11, 2009, from http://www.nga.org/Files/pdf/0806 TRANSPORTATIONTANIGUCHI.PDF

[21] Transek. (2006). *Equity effects of the Stockholm trial.* Retrieved February 11, 2009, from http://www.stockholmsforsoket.se/upload/ Sammanfattningar/English/Equity%20Effects%20of%20the%20Stockholm%20Trial.pdf.

[22] University of Minnesota & NuStats. (2005, March 4). *I-394 MnPASS project evaluation attitudinal panel survey final report.* Retrieved February 11, 2009, from http://www.mnpass.org/systemstudy.html

[23] U.S. Congressional Budget Office. (1990, August). *Federal taxation of tobacco, alcoholic beverages, and motor fuels: A CBO study.* Washington, DC. Retrieved February 11, 2009, from http://www.cbo.gov/ftpdocs/79xx/doc795 1/90-CBO-039.pdf

[24] U.S. Department of Transportation. (2008). *Report to Congress on the value pricing pilot program.* Washington, DC.

[25] Weinstein, A. & Sciara, G-C. (2004, November). *Assessing the equity implications of HOT lanes: A report prepared for the Santa Clara Valley Transportation Authority.* Retrieved February 11, 2009, from http:// knowledge.fhwa.dot.gov/cops/hcx.nsf/All+Documents/645B4DEABB1 3D7F085256FA30064485E/$FILE/ASSESSING%20THE%20 EQUITY %20IMPLICATIONS%20OF%20HOT%20LANES. pdf?OpenElement

# INDEX

## A



## B



## C

## D



## E



## F

## G



## H



## I



## J



## L



## M

## Y